These "new" poems by Peggy Pond Church complete the portrait of one of the American West's major (and too often overlooked) poets. In previous collections, Church masterfully and sensuously captured the Southwest: high, wind-swept mesas, spring orchards mid-bloom, moonlit Penitente processionals at Easter, the ominous advent of nuclear research at Los Alamos. Now, in these posthumously published works, Church turns her gaze upon herself, her family, and her friends. These are courageous personal poems. Sometimes shocking, often heart-breaking, they are never maudlin, saccharine, or sentimental. They leave us clear-eyed, sustained by their honesty and beauty.

—Tom Trusky, Ahsahta Press

For those who love the poetry of Peggy Pond Church and have yearned for more since her death in 1986, this volume is a long-awaited gift. *Accidental Magic* presents Church's life story, revealed in her sensitivity, humor, and perception of beauty while counterbalanced by her self-doubts and a sometimes haunting sadness. These poems are honest and deep.

—Sharon Snyder, Church's biographer

These poems ring with the forceful power of Peggy Pond Church's clear, strong, questioning "I/eye." One of the most cogent observers of the twentieth century, she unflinchingly renders the dilemmas of the modern world in poetic form. This selection will be a welcome resource in the ongoing reevaluation of literary modernism as well as an invaluable addition to the increasingly complex world of American women writers.

—Sarah Ann Wider, Professor of Literature, Colgate University

A smart and personally insightful and loving tribute to a poet whose stern self-criticism kept many of her poems from public view. Enhancing other Church collections, Kathleen Church helps us fully enjoy Peggy's oeuvre and stature—not only as a southwest writer but as an important figure in American poetry.

—Shelley Armitage, Peggy Pond Church literary editor
Oszagh Chair of American Literature, Budapest Hungary

Peggy Pond Church is a new testament in my religion of great poetry! She writes with such spiritual feeling and insight. It's like religion. I've been reading and reading *This Dancing Ground of Sky*…Its a poetic vision, everything between ground and sky! The discovery of new works of Peggy Pond Church is another stroke of *Magic* (What a beautiful title, from a beautiful poem opening "the door into a different dimension…") A poet's autobiography in her own poetry is i

—Jack Campbell, Professor

D0896778

Peggy Pond Church saw in nature and in people more than most of us saw. She is able to capture her vision in words, so that we, too, might see through her eyes.

–Kersti Tyson, Grand Niece
Joan Pond, Niece

accidental *Magic*

Peggy Pond Church

Book and cover design by Carolyn Kinsman
Cover photo collage by Judy Trujillo
Photographs from the Church family archives

Photographs in cover photo collage:

Front: Clockwise from upper left
Ashley III, Margaret (Peggy), and Dorothy (Dotty) Pond, c. 1912;
Camino Rancheros neighbor Ruth MacPherson and Peggy, c.
1980; Peggy, c. 1980; Hazel Hallett Pond, c. 1910; Peggy, c. 1960

Back: Clockwise from left
Peggy, Hazel, Dotty, Ashley, c. 1912; Fermor Church, c. 1944;
Peggy at signing for *A Rustle of Angels*, 1981; Peggy on Cochiti
Reservoir, 1983; Peggy at Otowi Bridge, c. 1980; Petroglyphs near
Galisteo, New Mexico; Virginia Wirth Wiebenson and Peggy near
Mt. Tschicoma, 1971; Hugh, Theodore (Ted), and Allen Church,
August 7, 1981, from *Sandia Lab News* article

Wildflower Press colophon designed by Sherri Holtke

Printed by Downtown Printing
Albuquerque, New Mexico

ISBN 0-9714343-6-0

The Wildflower Press

**P.O. Box 4757
Albuquerque, New Mexico 87196-4757**

Acknowledgements

Several of the poems in this collection were published during the author's lifetime. Grateful acknowledgement is made to the editors of the publications in which these poems first appeared. Gratitude is also extended to Sharon Snyder through whose research and persistence many of the poems came to light and were organized; to Judy Trujillo whose friendship and talent created the cover art; to Jeanne Shannon who guided and encouraged the production, and to Peggy Church herself, my mother-in-law, whose love I was happy to know and whose wisdom and beautiful words have been within me and beside me all these years. —KDC

Contents

1950s

1960s

1970s

accidental *Magic*

The Poem Cabin

Peggy's Poem Cabin built for her by her husband, Fermor, on the edge of Pueblo Canyon; her retreat during the Ranch School years.

Introduction

Though she and I exchanged our books of poetry and knew of one another, I never met Peggy Pond Church. Yet reading *Accidental Magic* makes me feel as though I were an intimate friend of a living person, so close to me is the spirit that hides and reveals itself as it finds its way through her poems. Her story is one other women can recognize as their own. At the same time, Peggy Pond Church's story chronicles an experience very few men and women in American history have undergone: her family, among several others, was displaced by the Manhattan Project in Los Alamos. She does not in this book make much of this. It matters no more and no less than her strongly felt reactions to accidental magic in her own life. It is that spirit which seems to me the particular gift of this book. She seems a living presence.

That some of the poems are unfinished and some are fragments, beginnings merely, cannot detract from the essential grace, intelligence, and truth of how she responds in her art to feelings evoked by her daily experience or deepened by her memory. Because the poems are chronologically arranged, it is possible to see how Church used the conventions of rhyme early on, while she was learning her craft by practice. Later, in keeping with contemporary change, she turned as readily to free verse as to rhyme. In both forms it is the sound of the language which engages her—alliteration, consonance and assonance, dissonance when she needs it—as well as an essentially rhythmic line wherein the syllable stresses fall musically.

Chronology is also responsible for some of the echoes of youth in later time. I think of the garden she planned in winter—"Poem for an Orchard Planting"—which evidently came into being—"The Garden." In this latter there occurs a telling image—the wisteria and the roses still alive beside the house the family had to leave—"in a city with numbered streets...and no one remembered Eden."

To my mind (and perhaps only because I myself am familiar with the experience), the strangest and strongest images occur in a poem called "Poet as Housewife," where the bird caught in her hand seems a metaphor for how she is hurt into poetry—"the neck a wrung child; / the cry a thorn's voice. / The egg twists in her / cool as a knife or a moon." Other images and themes strike me as being equally true, for example, "Rebellion" in which she writes of love's monotony, the need to make something happen, anything. Oh yes, I know about that. Especially I admire her candor in "Owl by the Rio Grande" as she speaks of her embarrassment at intruding on an owl, which, unseeing, erased her, "divested the air of my presence." I am moved also in a poem justly titled "Consummation" by the simplicity of how her husband asks, "Are you awake?" and offers her a drink of water in the middle of the night. That's a kind of tenderness I too recognize and appreciate. I am familiar also with the sense of talismanic change of a small stone carried up the mountain and down again ("Pilgrimage"), or the solid sturdiness, honesty, and comfort of a dirt floor ("Of the Dust of the Ground"), or the still image of a woman at prayer ("Oraciones").

These accidents of a life like my own, but not mine, seem magical to me. They give me the widened-out space of a life that makes my own deeper, richer, and, because Peggy Pond Church is so frank about her own life, easier for me to admit to. Finally, as she is the spirit of her poetry, as she is the essence of her life and being, she stands with me now, even after her death, as a dearly loved friend.

Phyllis Hoge Thompson
January 19, 2004

FOREWORD

Peggy Pond Church, author of *The House at Otowi Bridge*, a New Mexico classic, was first and last a poet. As a child who was shuffled from boarding school to summer camp to yet another boarding school, her consolation lay in a dream life which was reflected in her poetry. She meticulously kept and dated her early works, as she did most of the poems she wrote throughout her life until her death at eighty-two. Many poems were published in her several books: *Foretaste*, 1933; *Familiar Journey*, 1936; *Ultimatum For Man*, 1946; *New and Selected Poems*, 1976; *The Ripened Fields, Fifteen Sonnets of a Marriage*, 1978; *A Rustle of Angels*, 1981, and *Birds of Daybreak*, 1985. Seeking materials for a biography, Sharon Snyder and I have found nearly five hundred unpublished works. They turned up in file drawers, in letters, and tucked into journals. Some were marked "unfinished"; some were published only in a local newspaper or an obscure journal, and some were labeled "no" without explanation, but almost all carefully dated.

Peggy speaks of the importance of poetry to her in "Grief," published in *This Dancing Ground of Sky* (Red Crane Press, 1993):

> Poems ache
> in the heart
> the way stones do
> in an abdominal organ,
> stones
> that must travel a rough way
> to excretion.

Never easy, but always urgent, poetry was her life. Understanding this urgency, the need for this new volume of poetry has been nagging me since Peggy's biographer began cataloging the poems as she found them in the course of her research. Not all of them are here, of course; perhaps there will be another book. Interestingly, in 1977, Peggy wrote to Tom Trusky of Ahsahta Press, "The three books plus the sonnets contained most of the poems that were worth publishing. Well, maybe I could cull a dozen or so more." She was ever her own toughest critic and some of her best work came after 1977.

As I read through the unpublished poems, they seemed to resolve themselves into the pattern of an autobiography. Peggy's life is in this volume, the life of a remarkable woman living and prevailing at an intersection with the atomic age that changed her world and ours. From privileged but isolated childhood, to well planned self-extinction, the life of Peggy Pond Church reflects the events of Twentieth-Century America in the poetic lens of a New Mexican heart.

Kathleen D. Church
Albuquerque, New Mexico
January 2004

TO 1920

*P*eggy was born in December 1903; she was barely twelve when she wrote this first poem, "Ode to a Flower." She had grown up absorbing the fairy books of Andrew Lang, whose dedication in *The Green Fairy Book* says, "They [people long ago] believed that witches could turn people into beasts, that beasts could speak, that magic rings could make their owners invisible, and all the other wonders...." Peggy had spent hours and days alone or with her siblings, roaming the mesas and fields near her homes in New Mexico and Michigan. She had read the romantic stories of beautiful maidens, illustrated with *belle epoch* drawings. A difficult child of difficult parents, early in life she was sent off to one girls' school after another, seldom spending two years in the same school. From the age of six she was away from home during the school year, soothed during her loneliness by friendships and comforted by contemplation of nature. "Gabrielle" is addressed to her friend Gay Young-Hunter, the daughter of prominent Taos artists; "Sangre de Cristo" early expresses her loving observation of the New Mexican landscape, and "To A—" is the first of several poems to Aileen O'Bryan, who came to work at Los Alamos Ranch School in 1917 and triggered a girlish infatuation in Peggy's heart.

ODE TO A FLOWER

Long have I watched o'er thee,
Cared for thee, tended thee
  Through bright spring hours.

Now has thou burst into bloom
Laden with sweet perfume,
  Queen of all flowers.

Soon wilt thou fade away,
Queen of a summer's day,
  Withered, forlorn.

But I shall plant the seed
See to its every need,
  Till more flowers are born.

Francis W. Parker School, San Diego, California
February 1916

SANGRE DE CRISTO

Twilight over the mountains,
    Purple and gray and blue,
Whirl of a night bird's swooping wings,
    And breath of the evening dew.

Sudden a flash of crimson
    Sweeps up the mountain,
Red where the canyon shadows lie,
    Rose where the snow is white.

Watch! For the glow has deepened
    And gleams now a dark rose red,
Fading up to the mountain's crest,
    Leaving the foothills dead.

Dark are the purple mountains.
    Gray is the eastern sky.
Black are the depths of the air above,
    And the sunset colors die.

Pajarito Canyon, 1916

LULLABY

Hush, for the night-winds are calling, are calling,
    Sweet is their song.
Sleep till the dewdrops are kissed by the sunlight,
    It will not be long.
Dark is the night, but the stars are shining;
The dream-fairy waits for you over the sea,
And the sea is a sunset, the boat a dream.
    Sleep while I watch o'er thee!

Out of the hush comes a night bird calling.
    Low is his cry.
The firelight flickers while we are watching,
    Just you and I.
Drowsy your eyes, for the sandman is passing.
The dream-fairy calls to you soft and low.
Sleep—and wake with the morning glories
    Nor fear, for I will not go!

Hillside School, Norwalk, Connecticut
St. Nicholas League, Fall 1918

*The St. Nicholas League was organized by St. Nicholas
Magazine to promote intellectual advancement among
its readers. It awarded gold and silver medals in art and
writing. Winning entries were published monthly.*

GABRIELLE

There was a spray of blossoms in the room
Scenting the silvery dusk with sweet perfume,
And the hushed sound
Of music weaving magic through the gloom.
You dancing!
Music could not snare
Your radiant loveliness.
The glow of hair
Like shadows candle-lit.

> *Wabanaki School, Greenwich, Connecticut*
> *1918 or 1919*

TALE OF SPRING

There was a day in early Spring
When all the air was sweet with flowers,
    When rivers laughed and danced in play
    Over the rocks in rainbow spray,
Thru sunshine hours.

A wood nymph, crowned with dew buds,
Played with a dainty water sprite,
    And pelted her in merry glee
    With violets and ferns while she
Laughed with delight.

The water sprite, all dimpling, shook
Her long wet locks in happy play,
    Until the nymph, in sweet surprise,
    Dashed the bright drops from hair and eyes
And fled away.

Twilight it was in early Spring,
The deep clear pool was fringed with flowers,
      And dark and cool the shadow gleamed;
      The stream sang very low it seemed,
Thru shad'wy hours.

Hillside School, Norwalk, Connecticut
Silver Badge, St. Nicholas League, 1918

TO A—

I saw a rainbow laughing in the sky
And smiling in each April's drop of rain,
And so I caught them in my mirror's depths
That I might flash them on your heart again.

So if the skies are dark with rainy clouds,
Or if they hold all light within their blue,
Remember that my mirror's shining bright
To flash the old time rainbows back at you.

1919

1920s

*T*his decade saw continuing development in Peggy's life and in her poetry; her love of nature was already established in poems. She laid out the "Patterns" of her life in 1922, which then began to shift. Smith College life, with its occasional homecomings, held the charm of formal learning, but it was not enough to counteract the effects of meeting Fermor Church, a young master at Los Alamos Ranch School ("Your Room") who offered the opportunity of returning to the Pajarito Plateau. They were married in June 1924 and began life awkwardly as school resident teacher and wife. An almost immediate pregnancy and the school's intolerance for female influence meant Peggy would be more isolated than she liked. She did, however, have time to explore and enjoy the mesa ("Yesterday"), and she made time to think and to record her feelings. Her nostalgic poems, "Children Remember Knowing Aphrodite" (another poem about Aileen O"Bryan) and others retrieved the past. "Song for Airplane Flight" looked forward to the flying lessons she would take—a pioneer in aviation. "For Chauncey Hulbert" eulogized a young man who was a director at Camp Aloha in Vermont, and who died quite suddenly in young manhood. Peggy wrote the poem for his memorial service, establishing a pattern she would follow always of remembering with poems men and women whose lives and deaths touched her.

Two Santa Fe poems are here, and mixed in this section are the contentment of young motherhood, "Poem for Orchard Planting," and the restlessness that would later shake the foundations of her sanity and her marriage, "Rebellion" and "Pursuit."

PATTERNS

The sunlight weaves a pattern on the floor,
It shines across my books and through the door.
In the deep clearness of the morning hours
I see the fragrant rioting of flowers.

A pot of ivy on my mantel shelf
Is reaching upward like a twisted elf
Climbing into the sun. A candle's slim
Straight magic glows athwart my mirror's rim.

I wind my yarn and knit in even rows,
The while my needles click, and no one knows
How much the morning's tranquil beauty seems
To weave itself into my web of dreams.

Santa Fe
July 1922

HOMECOMING

It will be just the same. You'll say to me,
"Was the trip hard and don't you want to rest?
Tonight I'll get the supper." You'll have made
New curtains for my room. "They're nothing much.
Just some cretonne I saw the other day
And thought you'd like. Those pansies in your bowl
Nerissa brought. She knew you loved them best.
And dear," you'll say, in your old eager tone,
"The yellow roses have been all a-bloom
This month!" Thus it will seem somehow
As though I'd never been away at all,
To hear you talking in the same dear way
About your garden. So, when supper comes
There will be candles and the old blue cloth,
And zinnias rioting in the deep bowl
I sent you for your birthday. You will sit
Pouring the cocoa smilingly and say,
"It's good to have you home, dear. Would you like
Another cup, and is it sweet enough?"

Smith College
February 1923

YOUR ROOM

The rain
Was penciling thin lines across the sky,
Breathing a silver radiance through the trees,
Splashing its cool soft music on the roof
The day that I
Went with you to your room beneath the eaves.
I curled myself up in your window seat,
And kept my eyes upon the lifting curve
Of dim, sky-leaning hills.
You played "Thais"
On the small worn Victrola, and we two
Were very silent, knowing that one word
Might mar the beauty.
When I spoke
I told you all the whimsy of my heart;
How the wind made me feel that I could run
Soul-naked, silver-footed through the trees
Tangled with stars.
How sun-gold autumn leaves
Could thrill and burn the inmost depths of me,
While the gaunt mountain crags against the sky
Flung me resistless, reverent to my knees.

Summer 1923

FAIRY TALE

Time is a cavernous deep pool.
In it I drop the little jeweled hours
And listen to them splash far down,
A fairy sound, like petals dropped from flowers
Into still water.

Someday I'll slip into the pool myself
(For hours are precious things—
They're jeweled with dreams, come true!)
I'll find mine sparkling in the shadowy depths
And bring the loveliest ones all up to you.

Smith College
January 1924

RETURNING

You are so seldom with me through the day,
And yet I am not lonely though alone,
For all my thoughts go forth like petals blown
Across clear water. Far and far away
They widen seeking, snare in nets of spray
Color and light and sound and song unknown;
Beauty and life unsensed they make their own;
Shadows outside of time become their prey.

But it is the returning that is dear—
Thought-weary, when I come at last to you
Eager for quietness. Oh, draw me near
And comfort me as no one else can do
Until my restless thoughts that wander wide
Will leave me finally tranquil at your side.

November 1924

ENCHANTED

Perhaps I will take root here like the pines:
I have been still so long even the trees
Think I am one of them. That fragrant fir
Confidingly sets free her hidden birds.
The brown-clad oaks let fall their leaves in showers
And unashamed reveal their twisted forms,
Their bare unshapeliness. There is no sound
Save for the lulling of the lazy wind,
The buzz of flashing, iridescent flies,
The soft, sharp rustle of the blowing leaves.

I have no thoughts at all. The smallest pool
Of clear, unrippled water is aware
As much as I of wind and sky and leaves;
The way the shadows move, keeping the trees
Always between them and the seeking sun;
Of birds in cloud-high flight invisible
Save for that glint of sunlight under wing
Or silver throat.

Almost I am a part
Of the mute, age-old cliffs and silent hills.
Perhaps I will take root here like the pines,
I have been still so long.

October 1924
Southwest Review, *April 1925*

*Other titles for this often-reworked poem were
"Like the Pines" and "Perhaps I Shall Take Root."*

ESCAPE

She hid herself in a bird
That clung to a wire,
In a bird with tempestuous wings
And a throat of fire.

She hid herself in a cloud,
And she fell as rain
Musically on the grass
In a leaf-lit lane.

Oh, she was so grave and silent,
So shy of a single word,
That no one guessed she went swinging
On the wire in a bird.

None of us even missed her
Until we learned
She had fled in a leaf blown skyward
And had never returned!

July 1925
Poetry *magazine*

EIGHT YEARS OLD

Dusty and orchard-flanked and apple-sweet
Was the long road to town. A treeless hill
Held the small farm where they lived carelessly,
And where a child might run barefooted still.
These days she raced the wind on a swift horse
That knew his strength and scorned the tugging rein
Man pulled him with; ran like a thundering fire
Through empty fields, she clinging to his mane
With futile small brown hands. The great beast knew
That she was helpless as a storm-blown leaf
And he, as ruthless as a wind-wild storm,
Would fling her suddenly into the grass.
She would lie there unhurt a breathless while
Watching the brown fields blow and the clouds pass,
Then, still undaunted, trudge the dusty mile
That led to home. But there were other days
When she might ride him placidly to town,
And he'd wait patiently beside the road
If a cool fenced-in orchard pulled her down
To seek forbidden apples. Or would stand
Head-down in pasture cropping docilely
While she lay prone upon the reedy sand
And fished a sluggish stream with pin-hooked string
For tawny minnows. Once she ran away,
When she was temper-stung by some reproof,
Crying that she would not come back that day
Nor any other day her mother called.
She tramped through the hot fields all afternoon
With two tomatoes tied upon a stick
Across her shoulder, but when twilight came
Temper-defiance left her very soon.
Then hungrily and with a wistful shame
She hid awhile in the dim home-safe barn
Half longing to return and half to stay
In the warm darkness. Comfortingly near

The great horse calmly munched his evening hay,
Snorted a bit and stamped against the stall.
From the back door she heard her mother call
And went in half-afraid, yet eagerly
Hoping they'd be so glad to see her come
They would not scold the run-a-way at all!

March-April 1925
Children, the Magazine for Parents, 1927

SONG FOR AIRPLANE FLIGHT

I cannot make a cake;
I cannot sweep the floor,
though I darken the window
And though I bar the door.

For how long can dust disturb me
Lying on a chair?
Chair and dust are small things
Seen from blue air.

And how can I walk meekly
Preparing daily bread
Who have felt wind beneath me
And the sky at my head?

Body cannot bind me
To earth anymore
Who used to sit tethered
Watching spirit soar.

I have been lifted
On roaring wings
To the place where the moon hangs
And a bird sings.

And a house cannot hold me
Who have learned to fly
And know that sky is endless
And more than mountain high!

June 1925

THIRTEEN YEARS OLD

Was there no one at all but herself, no one at all
Aware of the terrible beauty of her world?
Was she the only one who heard it call—
That voice behind the stars, that song of the wind?
Did others see, perhaps, and hide their joy
As she hid hers, fearing someone would laugh,
Until her joy pent in a heart's close wall,
Destroyed itself with tears?

That thirteenth year
Was an uneasy, troublous time for her,
Full of strange questions. Began that tremendous stir
Of beauty in her heart that needed words
To sing itself, that needed singing words.
But she still had no words and had to bear
The ache unuttered.

She would sometimes run
Answering the wind's call, run along the stream,
Leaving her shoes behind; go splashing through
The cool, swift water. Sometimes around a rock
The water gathered in a tranquil pool
Waist-high to her. There as though half in dream
She'd lay her clothes aside on the warm grass
And play she was a naiad. Water was dim and cool,
Flecked by sun-shadows sifted through the leaves.

Sometimes she'd dance, shyly and half-afraid,
Like a wind-blown leaf on a sunny slope and still,
Warming herself in the sun. She would go back
Wordless at suppertime. She had no way
To tell the quiet ecstasy of her day
If any cared to hear. But no one cared,
Or so it seemed to her. Would it be always so,
She wondered, would there be anyone
Who would understand the way it made her feel—
Gloriously joyous, yet half-terrified
Of her strange thoughts?

She would kneel sometimes
Beneath her window when she went to bed,
Watching the stars shine in untroubled light
Beyond the sky. "Oh God, dear God," she'd pray,
"I can't quite find the words. Surely you know
The things inside my heart I want to say—"
Then she'd be still again, staring at the stars
As though she tried to drink them. After a while
She would go dreamily at last to bed
Almost asleep and strangely comforted.

1925

FOR CHAUNCEY HULBERT OF CAMP ALOHA

Lines written for Carol Hulbert

Surely he has not gone who always knew
So many ways of mastering the lake;
Who taught us all the swiftest ways to take
The windy water with our green canoe,
Or with sure-reaching arms to dive and break
The shining surface on warm summer days.

He has not gone who with us on the hill
Faced the sharp, silver challenge of the snow;
Who taught us how to guide our pointed skis
Past all the trees
And overtake the birds exultantly;
Showed us the winter thrill
Of racing, flying shadows in the glow
Of afternoon down a steep mountainside;
Or who at night
Entranced us with his story-teller's art,
Or showed us tricks to do around the fire
Or games to play.
He has not gone away!
Only we cannot see him for awhile
Or have the comradeship of that quick smile
He gave to all of us, or hear him tell
Those fireside stories that we loved so well.
But that strong spirit that made victory
Of all the things he did both great and small
Somehow lives on.
Perhaps a spark of it in all the hearts
He kindled some new joy of living in.
Thus will he still be climbing fern-fringed trails,
Or cleaving sun-swept water with us still
In some small eager boat with dipping sail,
Or riding horseback up a frost-bright hill.
Perhaps he has but gone ahead of us
Exploring some new trail and later on,
When we too find the path that leads us higher,
We'll overtake him, waiting by the fire!

1925

*Peggy attended Camp Aloha as a child, and she
and Ferm returned there as adult counselors.*

CHILDREN REMEMBER KNOWING APHRODITE

Never will violets spread their purple mist
Along a chanting stream, nor twinkling trees
Glow through their wind-mad leaves on a high hill.
Never shall we hear sky-spread melodies,
Or watch warm moonlight blow on summer grass,
Or see wild cherries bloom or white birds pass,
Or children dance except we think of you.

You were the goose girl of our storybooks,
Hair flying to the wind, and white bare feet,
Swift to run on the grass and through the brooks
And underneath the vines and hand in hand
With children treading over rippled sand.
We made believe we knew
That someday, if the fairy tale came true,
A prince would ride, mantled and plumed in green
And know you for no goose girl but his queen.

Silly, our mother said, to talk this way.
You ought to stay
And help us sweep and bake
Rather than run about the fields all day (with her).
They did not know how beautiful you were
With your earth-brown hair and twilight-colored eyes.
They only felt that you were magic wise
As the Pied Piper with all children's hearts
And feared you'd steal us from them.

Hush! we'd say,
She can take loveliness in her two hands (a leprechaun)
And hold it fast
No matter what disguise it wears to fright her!
We did not know (who were only children still)
That this was not a magic trick or game

But a way of grasping life to make it yield
At last the crock of gold (like the leprechaun).

She can make beauty grow, we said, on a bare wall,
Or a dusty sill, or anywhere at all
Where loveliness is latent. She can fly
Under a swallow's wing across the sky (we think)
Or show us a cloven print in the wet sand
Where a faun might lie
Under dripping leaves to watch a naiad bathe.

Always we think of gay things with your name:
The happy poise of your uplifted head;
The blue soft shadows of a curtained room;
And fairy tales; and children breaking bread;
The candle light on supper tables spread
Beneath a starry window; kitchen shelves
Bright-rimmed with painted cups; pictures of elves
And Arthur Rackham trees and blowing flowers;
The eager treasure hunts of little boys
And all pretend of childhood, broken toys
And bits of china hidden in a tree;
Strange tales of giants believed respectfully
By credulous grown-ups; all rain-splashed leaves;
All wind-bent grass and every sun-swept hill
To race great shadows in and finally spill
Laughing beside a berry-hidden wall;
The gold-drenched trails up mountain slopes in fall
Bring you back still.
(The lovely princess of our make-believe.)

For the fairy tale came true and the prince rode by
And found you (as we had dreamed)
with your wing-soft hair
Blown warm against the sky,
As bright a cloud
As any princess of the blood might wear.
And he has lifted you on his swift horse (we say)

And taken you far away. So we
Who have known more of you than he shall know
Can only have you for a memory.

And who can judge or who can truly know
How much of all we say of you was ever true,
Or how much only tales that children tell
Of some incarnate loveliness they knew?
It did not seem that you could ever go
Or that we could grow up. And music still
Tells us that on some far and lovely hill
You dance remembering.

April 1926

*Arthur Rackham (1867-1939) was a British illustrator of children's
books, famous for gnarled, anthropomorphic trees.*

YESTERDAY

Yesterday,
riding to Guaje,
a warm wind blew through the spruce boughs.
The snow ran in rivulets to the river.
Above the yucca shone a vision of flowers.

Yesterday,
riding to Guaje,
I saw trees mighty in girth, tall and cool-shadowed,
rooted in a black dome of rock once molten.
I saw the river
bent from its course at the place
where the canyon is narrow,
flowing between the dark cliffs.

Yesterday,
in a canyon beyond Guaje,
I saw a deer flee through the pines.
I heard the wind on a mesa beyond
stride furiously from the mountain.
I saw swift clouds
darken the sun.
I heard the advancing rain.

At a cliff's edge I saw a ruined city
whose name is now forgotten.
There were five kivas carved in the hard rock;
forgotten now
are they who fashioned prayers.
Not even high-flying birds remember these walls,
only the high-spread stars.

It is long in men's memory since these cities stood
white in the sun.
Yet even then had the river carved this canyon
and the far-off valley remembered in these same shadows
the colors of an ocean.
Thus yesterday reaches backward and forward forever
and disappears like the sky.
How can I say what I thought while riding to Guaje
yesterday?

1926

*Guaje is a canyon, one of several cutting through the Pajarito
Plateau, about two hours by horseback north of Los Alamos.*

26

SANTA FE

We cannot sell
The beauty of our city for a coin.
Nor make a market-place for loveliness
Where loveliness is bred. We have awakened
Who might, perhaps, have thought no more about it
Another time of year. We can be sure
That in no other city would we find
Fruit trees by almost every blue-silled door.
Nor any other place where stars may shine
Serene, undimmed, above the city lights.
Are we content to have our trees give way
To flimsy houses—houses without trees?
Would men plant orchards for a summer's length,
Or carry water to them in a drought
By weary bucketfuls?
                        Be warned, be warned
By all the exultant clamoring of spring—
Let not the bloom be ravaged lest the tree die
And no more fruit hang ripened from the bough!

                The Santa Fe New Mexican *and*
                Literary Digest, *June 1926*

OH, I WAS ALWAYS SPEAKING

Oh, I was always speaking
A gay and valiant word
To hide the dread within my heart
From anyone that heard.
And I was always hiding
From anyone's surmise
The window where my soul looked out
With cool, ironic eyes.

                November 1926
                The New Yorker

REBELLION

Some days I'd like to scream; or smash a vase;
Or hurl a saucepan through the window-pane;
Show anger in a hundred different ways—
By tears; or temper; running in the rain
Without my hat on—anything to be
A thing I am not every usual day!
I'd like to get *you* very angry at me
So I could scream, and stamp the floor, and say
I know you did not love me!

But then you
Would never understand the reason why
I'd say a thing so scathingly untrue,
And you'd be hurt and bitter; you'd not see
My need of uttering that one blasphemous lie
To shake my soul from love's monotony!

1926

PRAYER

Let me live keenly as a lark high-soaring
In one swift arc of song across the sky;
However brief let my flight be unswerving
And straight and high.

Or let me flow toward the end of being
Silver and sure as mountain water flows;
Nor ever wait in stagnant pools or marshes
Where no wind blows.

Let me increase as rivers do and gather
Wisdom from hills and every rooted tree;
Then let me go at last like quiet water
Toward the sea.

August 1926

ORACIONES

In the blue doorway
Lupita sits sunning
Herself for a moment.
The beads through her fingers
Slip half-forgotten;
Her prayers are as soft
As the ring of small bells
Ascending heavenward
With smoke from the fire
That is fragrant with cedar
And the perfume of apples
In the sun-mellowed orchard
Beyond the acequia.

September 1928

POEM FOR A DANCER

Pause one moment
In captured ecstasy.
Hold loveliness in your spread arms.
Trace beauty
With the arched body, with the poised white thigh.
Be wind, be music, be the delicate foam
On the uplifted wave.
Oh dance my own mute longings and my dreams
On the sea-trodden sand.

October 1928

POEM FOR ORCHARD PLANTING

I will plant an orchard for my children;
Though it is winter
And the ground is white and frozen,
A mirror for the black shadows of crows flying above it,
Still I am thinking of an orchard for my children
As soon as the ground is warm, as soon as the snow
Runs in a thousand finger-printed
Pathways to the river.

I will have peach-trees first.
And how shall I ever wait
The spring of their blooming
Mad, vivid, blinding among white clouds of plum?
How shall I ever wait the year when blossoming comes
First to my pear-tree, waxen and tall as candles?
Apples I must have
For the fragrance of fruit and blossom,
The warm heavy fragrance of flowers
In spring, in the moonlight;
Of the fruit in the summer.

Even now I can dream:
Now while the snow is white on the frozen ground,
Of my daughter's brown head
Haloed in a mist of cherries;
Of the shaken leaves of a branch above me walking,
And a voice calling,
Calling from fruit-stained lips.

Even now, before I have set
The slip of one tree in the ground
And patted it with my spade and hallowed around it
A basin for cool water, I can see far up,
Far up in the branches
Where the fruit hangs heavy
My son, who is not yet three,
With the wind under him;
The wind under him and on his face a dream.

I will set out an orchard for my children
As soon as the sun swings southward
And the ground warms.

1928
Children, The Magazine for Parents

PURSUIT

Do not laugh at me. Do not call me morbid
Because in the midst of life I hear death running
Hot on my trail, hungering at my footprints.

If death did not pursue I might grow careless,
Might not watch so closely, wait so eager
On each leaf-opening, forget to look at mountains.

Do not laugh at me, nor call me morbid
Because I think of death as a tiger waiting
To drop on me like a silence from forest branches.

I am the faster now. I can outrun him.
When I, growing weary, stumble, then he may have me:
They find life most beautiful, fearing it suddenly ended.

May 1929

1930s

A momentous decade! The last of Peggy and Ferm's three sons was born in 1932. This was Hugh, preceded by Allen and Ted, the oldest. Three books were published: *Foretaste* (1933), *Familiar Journey* (1936), and a children's book, *The Burro of Angelitos* (1936). The poetry books were published by Santa Fe Writers' Editions, "a cooperative group of writers living in the Southwest, who believed that regional publication will foster the growth of American literature." The Writers' Editions venture is now regarded as unique in publication history, and the books are highly valued.

There was also a nervous breakdown: "On a Night of Despair," a love affair, and a reconciliation, "Consummation." Nearing the end of the decade after all the emotional upheaval, Peggy relaxed a bit, taking aim in her poetry at the exaggerated masculine regimen demanded by the director of Los Alamos Ranch School, A. J. Connell, in "Some Lines Suggested for a Boarding-School Prospectus."

MATER DOLOROSA

Heavy am I now, with sorrow,
As though I carried my child still under my heart;
Swollen these breasts
with the milk that cannot cease flowing,
And the nipples that ache for lips once warm and eager;
Swollen my heart with love no longer needed.

Sharp, far sharper than the pain that rent me
When I first heard his cry, his thin, small wailing,
It is to hear this small cry stilled forever;
To give back to the womb of the earth-mother
This child my own womb has not yet forgotten.

For F.W.P. February 26, 1931

*This was probably for Peggy's school friend
who lived in Maine.*

FOR MY MOTHER, WHO CLAIMS
THAT I HAVE NEVER WRITTEN
A POEM TO HER

There is a picture I have of you that I love
taken when you were sixteen, a picture in profile,
a proud and delicate profile, abundant hair
piled high on a small head,
the head posed firmly,
a velvet ribbon about the slender throat,
determined chin, lips curved and not quite smiling,
wide candid eyes.
Oh very demure and made for lace and ruffles,
and I smile to remember how you used to be the scandal
of all your neighborhood when you were little
because you cut off your hair and dressed in bloomers
and played with the boys

34

and threw ripe figs at the little girls you hated,
and rode your pony astride up all the hillsides,
and never would be a lady.

I remember that you bore your first child at eighteen
in a New Mexico ranch house,
and that your mother wasn't with you,
and that you had driven
twenty-five miles that day in a buckboard
to bring a nurse from the city
and that it was a long labor and a hard one
and your mother wasn't with you,
and the child was not the boy you had wanted but a girl
and born a month too early
and the December wind was cold in the stunted cedars.

And I remember how not a year later
the little creek suddenly swelled with the autumn rains
and when you woke in the night
the water was ankle-deep in your bedroom.
You wrapped a blanket around you
and wrapped the child in its blankets
and my father took you through the storm
to a barn on the hillside
where you lay all night shivering, listening to the water
roar from wall to wall of the little canyon.
In the morning you were driven to the village in a wagon,
passing on the way a wagonload of dead bodies.
You had only a blanket around you
and that was all you had left in the world.
The rest the stream had taken.
You were only nineteen then.

And I remember
the dozens of homes you made for us,
you who were married to a wanderer and a dreamer,
an expander of horizons who thought
that what he was seeking
lay always over the next hill or over the next river.

You made a home once
in one room, cement floored, built for a garage first,
on a hot hill without trees,
but even there your garden blossomed
and your children had shade to play in,
flowers on the table and monogrammed silver,
and the old clock that had stood once on a stately landing
in a luxurious house in a luxurious city.

You never accepted
the strange gods of an alien soil.
You, like your mother and grandmother before you,
carried your own traditions with you
wherever you went, your own gods, your own traditions,
rooted them fiercely
in each inhospitable wilderness you were asked to inhabit.

And there were many roofs and many walls,
but between the walls always the same home;
the memory of them blends in my mind.
I cannot remember
all the separate rooms; there was a wide verandah
that looked over a lake once where I used to sleep,
and a nursery, cool and dark in summer
that I came into with my bare feet hot from running
on the warm sand at the lake's edge,
on the warm grass at the hill top.
Later a far away window
and beyond the window a pine tree
and Cassiopeia's Chair, and the Sword of Perseus,
and Andromeda, familiar patterns
pricked on the dark sky in summer.
There was a white room once
with a deep window and a fireplace,
a fireplace all my own across one corner,
the smell of cedar sticks burning there in winter,
and a gray kitten
that slept at the foot of my bed, the wandering
tendrils of ivy in the pot beside the window.

Many roofs, many walls, but always
the dignity, the security, the order
you enclosed within your walls like one soul
that is incarnate again and again in different bodies,
a dream giving shape to itself, a dream you gave shape to
over and over. The floods could not drown it.
Time could not destroy it. It has not crumbled
with any crumbling walls.
And now you build it once more,
and once again the dream calls forth a garden
out of a bare slope, out of a dusty weed patch.

I have a picture of you
that I love. Deep in my heart I have it,
a picture you gave me, a dream that you made for me
that I build now into the walls of my own life.

June 1934

OH, NIGHT OF DESPAIR

Oh, night of despair—
and I walked under a wide-ringed moon,
under a ghostly sky,
and the mountains shimmered.
Lightening blossomed again and again
and shook off its petals.
I walked down a dirt road.
I walked down a brick side-walk.
Under the street lights I lowered my head
and looked downward
lest any should see I was weeping.

Oh night of despair—
the poplars mad with the shaken wind,
and I walking,
shaken with grief like the poplars,

thinking of the one I could not love
and how I had wounded him,
thinking of his love
that had been safe bulwark about me,
weeping because I could not love him,
weeping.

The dark houses I passed,
and the lighted ones,
the people talking beside their fires,
or weeping,
and I walking the dark streets alone with heartbreak.
How many heartbreaks were hid in the still houses?
How many walked the dark streets?

And I passed the house of my brother,
oh, more than my brother.
I stood outside the gate of the walled garden
and thought I should go in and ask him for water,
only a cup of water.
The lightning blossomed
and shook off its petals a thousand times
while I stood there
weeping and praying.

At last I turned and went back
the long way, the windy way,
under the turbulent trees, under the shimmering clouds.
Why should I lay the weight of my heavy heart
upon my brother?
But if I had opened the door
I would have found him walking there,
my brother who is more than my brother,
walking in his garden under the petals of lightning,
holding my heart upon his heart.

May 26, 1934

CONSUMMATION

Folded still in my dream I seemed to waken
as though out of long sickness, out of long delusion,
to find my fever gone. I lay and listened
to a childhood sound of sheep. I heard an owl cry
once, twice. I heard you move beside me,
but still in dream. Are you awake? you asked me.
Would you like a drink of water?
and poured it for me from the pitcher on the table.
I drank. It was as though a miracle
had blossomed in my hand, a rose in winter
or water from the rock in wilderness.
at the tip of Moses' rod. Oh lost in endless desert
blackened with thirst I came to this crystal fountain
and drank, and plunged my face into the living water
and then in joy I laid my hand upon you
and felt under my hand the warm bud quicken.

Oh, love! I cried. And with this cry I wakened
and knew I had come home!

June 1, 1934

LOVE SONG IN WINTER

This weight of white, these plumed wings,
this feather-breasted, ancient bird
comes down upon us like a dream,
comes on us like a blessed word.

The fir tree bends its arched branch
low to the ground, oh, low and still,
and not a wind can pierce this web,
and not a sound come nigh this hill.

Now you and I in folded sleep
lie breast to breast and quietly,
your hands like wings against my hair,
your knee above my naked knee.

And here we sleep as children sleep
unwakened yet from the dark womb:
thou, brother to my heart, and I
your sister in a single doom.

And we shall wake when term is spent,
and we shall rise and softly go,
and tread as light as angels tread
across the silent, stainless snow.

December 1935

SOME LINES SUGGESTED FOR A
BOARDING-SCHOOL PROSPECTUS

Behold the adolescent boy,
the nascent youth, the budding man.
'Tis now he must be disciplined
and governed by a stable plan.
He sprouts like some ungainly weed,
with food and drink he must be plied.
His greatest needs are those that feed
the biological inside.
Oh, stuff him well and shelter him;
a strong physique he must attain;
with rest and lots of exercise
build bone and brawn and blood and brain.

And if he steals away to brood
Oh, follow him and bring him back.
'Tis very uncooperative
and shows a grave, unmanly lack.
His soul must don our uniform.
No difference will be allowed;
no individualistic trait
to mark him out among the crowd.
He must conform in all his ways.
If he does not, beyond a doubt
this mass-productive stream-lined age
will turn on him and cast him out.

And since the female of all sex
it is which causes tears and strife,
we'll solve the problem here and now
by expurgating it from life.
No bitches may disturb the peace
among our canine population.
No restless mare may here abide
to cause our geldings mild vexation.

And if ourselves should choose to wife
why wives may come and they may sit
in little harmless hennish groups
apart from us and chat and knit.

For man it is must rule the world
but womanishness will not let him.
We'll wall the boy away from it
lest it should here intrude and fret him.
No thought that smacks of feminine,
no dark emotionality
shall threaten here his manly mien
nor stir his equanimity.
If he will stay awhile with us
we'll make him into something human
that bears no more the horrid trace
of having once been born of woman.

March 1939

*A. J. Connell, school Director, had a very ugly dog he
named Peggy–perhaps in reaction to such jibes.*

1940s

*P*eggy's marriage now assured, she examined the nature of her intimate relationship with Ferm, usually in sonnet form. Religious and spiritual issues surfaced. Peggy and Ferm had studied *Teachings From the Life of Jesus;* their inherited Episcopalian experience was set aside for Quaker practice. Her spiritual thoughts involved the dualities, cycles of life, and the blind, unacknowledged response of mankind to nature. Many poems at this time were published in *Inward Light,* a Quaker journal. These were often her sonnets on marriage. The demanding sonnet form intrigued her, and she practiced it as she analyzed her marriage. The ultimate result would be *The Ripened Fields: Fifteen Sonnets of a Marriage* (1978), a collection begun at this time and developed through the years.

Of course, the decade was a time of wars. Some of Peggy's strongest responses came in poems published in *Ultimatum for Man* (1946), thus not included in this collection. Her anger, however, is evident in "Alas, I Know" and "Anno Domini, 1947." World War II led to eviction for the Churches when The Manhattan Project commandeered the Ranch School, closing it. Many poems from this time on reflect the loss of a golden time of freedom. "Of the Dust of the Ground" describes their new home in Taos, including the search for earthy values—for essential verities in a time of chaos.

Often overlooked in discussions of Peggy's work is her sense of humor, charming by contrast with somber, deep thoughts. It appears in this decade in poems like "To Edward Weeks, Editor of *The Atlantic Monthly*" and "Bean Is My Shepherd."

SONNETS FOR A MARRIAGE

I.

Twice ten years you and I have striven now
as though we were two hands that clenched and fought
and parried and repelled. On neither brow
the wreath of victory rests, yet we have bought,
with price of this our sweat and these our tears,
dearer than victory, the struggle's end.
Our eyes at last unbandaged of old fears
behold the enemy for more than friend.
Now like two hands unclenched we clasp or fold
as mated hands upon the left and right
of one great being must; or, opened, hold
the task he labors on, and day and night
we are his hands. We are his fingers skilled
in opposite form to bless, to bind, to build.

October 18, 1943

II.

Why do I weep against your heart at night?
I weep that summer ends, and that my pride
possessed my nature as a demon might
So that I am your long belated bride.
I weep for the heart cased in glass or ice,
the seed in rind so long that would not yield,
the treasure hoarded for a fabulous price,
the grain unsprouted in the frozen field.
I weep for bloom begrudged when spring was young.
Now buds and leaves from barren branch have sprung
and lo! The stars of winter edge the sky.
We must live all four seasons in this one
whose love has blossomed in an autumn sun.

October 21, 1943

44

III.

There are no words for this deep mystery,
this conversation of the hand, the thigh,
the breasts that melt beneath your leaning weight
so that our two hearts fuse. My heart enfolds
your beating heart as though our flesh, our bone
were pervious to love. This is the full
and strange reversal of maternity.
You are become my child. You pierce my flesh
and enter back into the silent place were life waits
unbegotten. You have come
through all the barriers to my naked heart.
Communication on this beyond all word,
this inward sense that is not speech nor tongue
nor beauty loving eye, this pure, this bare
touch upon life's great pulse that two may share.

                                    November 2, 1943

OF THE DUST OF THE GROUND

She said, raising a fastidious brow,
Your floors are made of dirt!
Yes, made of dirt, I said,
of earth mixed well with straw
that once was a sunned field
mellowed and rotted to pliability
by the skilled chemistry of rain.
An old man, laughing, mixed it,
stirred dirt and water to an almost fluid
boggy consistency, carried it in pails
indoors. An old woman laid it
deftly smooth between four white walls,
kneaded and leveled it and smoothed it,

with only a skilled eye to measure it,
only two good firm hands to marry it
to the hard ribs of earth beneath.
She washed it often
with water and grimy piece of
sheep's wool, pressed it harder, firmer,
gave it a gently rounded
slightly irregular and female contour.
Yes, they are made of dirt,
my floors. They say the Lord God
formed man of the same stuff.
I walk upon them
reverently, most often without shoes,
feeling the holy oneness of all living.

My visitor's lifted eyebrows
frowned still, spurning still the humble
dust-colored texture of my floors.
I think her ashes
will rest in a cold urn, well mausoleumed,
for centuries after mine have joined the living
passionate texture of earth,
and greet the morning
with unquenchable recognition.
She shall rest there
among the dead, never to be reborn
until she mingles
her dust with the earth's dust.

Autumn 1944

*Indeed, Peggy's (and Ferm's) ashes rest in Garcia Canyon,
part of the "texture of earth." That location is now a
restricted area on Santa Clara Pueblo land.*

POET AS HOUSEWIFE

Bird, a fire of blue feathers
in my prison-fingered hand;
the wing, weak as a severed angle,
punishes the anvil of my wrist;
the neck a wrung child;
the cry a thorn's voice.

The egg twists in her,
cool as a knife or a moon.
Her nest is a mouth or a whirlpool,
her breast is a coal of midsummer.
She is a tornado
fierce as a motherhood of lions or thistles.

She beaks my finger
and brings blood,
I in a woe to save her
with this kitchen-cup of a stone's tears,
the eggs splintered like flowers,
the sun split.

One eye of silver
swims in the black and single
whirl of the healed nest.
Oh how can I consent her now to cradle,
her wing a wreath, her breast a lens of rainbows
among my salads and my sacraments?

TO EDWARD WEEKS, EDITOR OF *THE ATLANTIC MONTHLY*

Box K, Taos, New Mexico
March 13, 1945

Dear Mr. Weeks:

I shot four sonnets into the air.
They fell to earth I knew not where,
although they were addressed with care
    to The Atlantic Monthly
    8 Arlington St., Boston, Mass.

The days sped past. The weeks went by.
The months did plod I'd hoped would fly.
The postman brought me no reply
    not even my self-addressed envelope
    not even my uncancelled air-mail stamp.

Long afterward, in fact next year
my long lost poems did reappear
with graceful editorial tear.
    (I'm sure Mr. Weeks is the kind of
    man who says to his children when he
    spanks them, "This hurts me much more
    than it does you.")

I'm puzzled now how poets do earn
enough to make their home fires burn
when editors so late return
    their handiwork with nothing to show
    for so many idle months but an extra,
    though to be sure, highly valuable
    paper clip.

But all facetiousness aside, I am most grateful for your
criticism and respect the accuracy of your judgment of the "rigid
dissonant quality of many of my lines." I am also
trustfully submitting a new poem to the tender mercies of
The Atlantic, whose rejections often increase determination
and competence more than a brisk acceptance ever could.

Sincerely,
Mrs. Fermor S. Church

INDIAN SUMMER

I am more desperate, more alone than I can say.
We have lived so close, and yet so far apart.
You have armored yourself in routine of every day.
You have hidden your thought from me, and all your heart.
Now round and round the close-chinked wall I go
and weep and tear my hands, yet cannot find
among the quarried stone piled row on row
the smallest entrance to your heart, your mind.

And though I cry my heart upon the air,
only the echo of my voice returns,
waking no harmony against the bare
and adamant bastions. No tender ferns
or delicate ivy clings upon that wall.
No secret door swings open at my call.

August 1945

ALAS, I KNOW

How easy it is to say,
"If earth were purged of all my enemies
then I would worship God in my own way
and be at peace."

See, evil is so ranged on every hand
that I must stand
a lamb among ferocious lions of fate,
nations that fight each other, men who hate,
doom that towers cloudlike on the helpless sky.
So day and night with trembling voice I cry
against the shape of murder in my land.
I cry that earth make peace that I may live.

Alas, I know
the world is but the mirror of my heart.
God made it one,
but I divide it daily, bid the sun
shine upon those I love, bid evil rain
on those I dare not love.
As long as I still hold the world apart
in my own breast for any fear or gain
how can I hope that others shall lay down
their enmities?
I come before God's throne,
the father of all men, and cry for peace,
yet will my brother's death before my own.

Fellowship *(a Quaker Journal)*

ANNO DOMINI, 1947

Let us remember this year—
only how we have shamed Him
in whose honor our gifts were once given,
Let those who are without sin make merry.
Let whosoever knows
that his brother has nothing against him
offer his gift with a whole heart upon the altar.

We who still feast at the inn
shall have lights of all colors and yards of tinsel
and a juke box to drown out the voice of any angel.
The star in the east will be imitated in neon,
and, that late travelers may understand
              the situation clearly,
the no-vacancy sign will be flood-lit.

Some will come to the feast perhaps a little breathless
because of trouble along the road.
"A woman we met seeking a place
              for her child to be born in.
She seemed to be without a country.
No nation would claim her,
Someone will have to determine what zone she belongs in
before her case can be handled."

There was a disturbance, too, outside the stable
that has been set aside as a shrine. Some wild fanatic
overturned the counters of those who have concessions
to buy and sell there—for the sake, of course, of tourists.
We heard him mutter some rigamarole about "prayer,"
              and "all the nations"
before we locked him up.

It is a pity that things like this can happen
on the very eve of Christmas.
A man can hardly travel from Jerusalem to Jericho
these days without encountering someone
who has fallen among thieves;
there are steps that should be taken.
In the meantime, let us proceed to open
the gifts we have been given
thanking God tonight that we are not as others.

A Christmas poem signed "Ferm and Peggy Church"

BEAN IS MY SHEPHERD

*"At times you will feel sure your compass is wrong. The best way to
overcome this feeling is to carry two compasses."*
From the Catalog of L.L. Bean

My prophet for this modern scene
is L.L. Bean
who through life's woods in sun or snow
will outfit me to go
in featherweight attire most safely pent
from any element.

I wear Bean's shoes upon my either feet,
both waterproof and neat.
I carry all my comforts at my back
in Bean's approved pack,
and bed myself upon, when I'm all in,
Bean's rubber tarpaulin.

Armed with Bean's axe whose most commended grace
is to reflect my face,
dangling Bean's feathered minnow in my hand,
serene I stand
in this confused world, equipped with lure
infallible and sure.

Naught shall affright me. Have I not Bean's word
through all dilemmas heard?
Though lost in wilderness my wild surmise
is that Bean's compass lies.
I'll not despair. The obvious thing to do,
says Bean, is carry two.

The poem, originally printed in The Atlantic *in July 1949,
was reprinted in L.L. Bean's 75th birthday "scrapbook,"
accompanied by an ad for Bean's Maine Woods Compass
in the fall 1937 catalog.*

1950s

*I*n the 50s the comfort and friendships in Taos widened. "Thumbnail Sketch" depicts Frieda Lawrence, a Taos icon and wife of D.H. Lawrence. "Andrew's Tree" was part of a memorial service for Andrew Dasburg, the important modern artist, and the Churches' neighbor. In many poems of this period, Peggy brooded about her family's lost life on the plateau. "Orders" reflects her emotions when Allen, her middle son, was drafted, and "Los Alamos" addresses the family's feelings as displaced persons. "The Whiffenpoof Pool" recalls a story she and her young siblings had believed. Life went on; the family expanded; all three boys married, and grandchildren were born: "Nancy at the Airport" and "Robyn's Birthday." "For M," written for May Sarton, is one of a few poems reflecting Peggy's continuing relationships with other renowned poets. "Powamu" is a powerful plea for unity and peace in a time of violence.

In 1956 Ferm took an engineering job in California, and the Churches moved to Berkeley. Peggy continued work on *The House at Otowi Bridge*, which she had begun five years earlier. It would be her major life work in poetic prose. Their life seemed full and positive, but the sense of loss remained. "Stand Thou" reverberates with the effort to suppress her own willfulness and achieve peace.

ORDERS

Today your orders came.
We had been expecting this,
but somehow it fell like a stern blow,
like the closing of a door, like a key turning,
like footsteps departing.
Now, the anonymous millions marching
and falling through the pages of history,
statistics in newsprint,
suddenly merge into one, and the face of
the vulnerable heart is your heart.

We remember your childhood,
the flowers pulled in the garden,
the willow tree shaken, the music you loved,
the strings of fish you came home with;
beautiful as a wild thing, beguiled as a young faun
at your own image, generous as summer,
you must be taught now
to hate and to wield death.

Wield death, if you must then and under orders,
but do not hate, my son. The body can be commanded
but not the heart's fruit. Death is a transition,
but hatred corrupts the living like a worm in the ripe fruit.
Render to Caesar nothing that is not Caesar's;
the right to love can be mastered no more than heartbeat
or the warmth of a fire or the perfume of roses at evening.

December 6, 1950

LOS ALAMOS

I dreamed we went, as once we used to go,
horseback across the mountain-high plateau
where once the wind was a transparent sea
breaking in brightness over every tree,
pouring its light upon the golden grass
where we as children saw the wild deer pass,
and heard the turkey call, and the soft dove
intone her gentle memory of love.

Once more, in dream, our eager horses strode
the homeward winding, summer-dusty road,
the saddle leather warm between our knees,
the steaming sweat, the aromatic trees,
the sharp, quick ring of hooves, the shaken manes,
the supple tension of the bridle reins;
Oh, hand and heart and mind in unison,
the horse's wisdom and the man's made one!

Now all save this was changed. The road we knew
came to a gate and no one could pass through
who did not swear to look nor left nor right
and to forget whatever threatening sight
might meet his wayward glance. Stricken, we stayed
until our claims to enter could be weighed
by guard whose face was frozen in a frown.
We looked within and saw the trees cut down,
and saw a city stand, and saw men there
given what they might ask to make life fair,
houses they had not built, and water towers,
effortless playthings for their leisure hours,
streets where the smallest child might safely run,
churches with tall spires gleaming in the sun,
yet every face there wore, it seemed to me,
the look of creatures in captivity.

No man sang his own song. No children cried,
"Run, Sheep! Oh run, Sheep, run!" at eventide.
The soda fountain flowed; the jukebox played.
Dogs, tethered, still felt wildness, sometimes bayed
the invisible moon; hardly a man at night
looked up to see the stars' remembered light.
None called his house his own when day was done,
and no man loved the task he labored on,
nor looked with joy upon his own child's face
so innocent of harm still in that place
where each man wove, in barred and secret room,
some small fierce portion of his neighbor's doom.
    Our patient horses stood with dragging rein
    but time would not turn back for us again,
    nor take the stain of terror from those skies
    nor give us back our dream of Paradise.

July 1, 1950
El Crepusculo

During the Manhattan Project and until the February
of 1958, all homes were owned by the government.
Government-built homes were sold to inficiduals in 1965.

THE WHIFFENPOOF POOL

If you go forth on a midsummer night
you may catch, if you wait till the moon is right,
and if you hunt him all alone
a whiffenpoof for your very own!

Now the things you will need to take are these:
a raft, an auger, and a piece of cheese.
You must hold your breath and make never a sound
till you come to a pool that is perfectly round,

that is perfectly round as a silver plate,
and there you must watch and there you must wait
till the full moon stands at the top of the sky
and looks at the pool with her wide round eye.

Then you must push with raft and pole
to the pool's exact middle and bore a hole
as narrow and straight as an arrow's flight
and not a hair's breadth to the left or right.

On the top of the hole you must place the cheese
and wait till you see the whiffenpoof squeeze
up through the hole that is tight for him
even when hungry and perfectly slim.

He will look to the left, he will look to the right
and gulp the cheese in a single bite;
then gorged and full he will find with pain
he cannot get down the hole again.

So he will be yours to have and hold,
for such is the tale my grandsire told,
and I've only been *waiting* this many a night
for the pool to be round and the moon to be right!

1950

*This is signed "Peg ass us," often used on humorous
childhood poems.*

SONNET XVI

Who are you whom I seek east of the sun,
west of the moon, whose spirit must be freed
and waked to know your true bride? I have come
a long, long journey, past the clutching reed,
the icy mountain and the sharpened spears.
At every door I gave some jewel in fee
to the stern guardian. Naked now, in tears,
I wait outside your door. Oh speak to me
in your own voice. I know not if you are
swineherd or prince, but that you are my own.
On the long journey you were the fixed star
in the abyss of heaven thickly sown
with shifting shapes of stars. My destiny
to seek you through all shapes and set you free.

February 1951

THUMBNAIL SKETCH

Sitting at Frieda's feet at the cocktail party
I liked the strong feel within her of her long life,
like a river not far from the sea and calmly flowing,
full of its tributaries, its gathered sources,
mountain lands, meadow lands, the change of season,
all that this life has been looking out through her calm eyes,
all life she has been part of transfigured in her,
and the child she still is embracing the wise old woman.

November 1951

ANDREW'S TREE IN THE MOONLIGHT

Andrew's tree in the moonlight is like a fountain,
a fountain that slowly, slowly, through the long years
thrusts upward out of the burst seed. Every round leaf
is a fragment of light or life that rains through the pale air
as though a fountain were arrested in mid-motion.
The crown of this tree is like the arch of the rainbow
bending toward the earth, or like the embrace of a mother
over her sleeping child. The strong surge of the branches
upward has reached its full height. Now slowly, slowly,
the lines of all motion turn downward.
Each stem is weighted toward earth now.
Moonlight in our eyes reflected
from the branches of Andrew's tree is an incarnation
of light in the shape of life, the living, the dying,
balanced in unison like sound, like silence,
of which all song is made. Summer and winter
this tree has been our time mark. In our mind's eye
we see it in all its stages, green on the bare boughs,
at one with the presence of white snow,
with the gold leaves,
with the mockingbird's song remembered.
The children we have been
lift their arms to these branches,
shuffle through the dry leaves,
rest, hot from play, in the sweet bounty of shadow,
the underside of light. Our joys, our sorrows,
are aromatic as the mold on which these roots feed,
mortal as leaves, immortal in their dying,
enriching the heart's blood still. The sap leaps upward
forever toward the sun. Andrew's tree in the moonlight
is more than a tree; has become for a space a vision
in which we behold all trees, all times, all seasons,
all loves, all deaths; our own ascent and returning
from darkness to darkness, and the light reflected
in wonder from our eyes. Andrew's tree is a fountain

in which time is born and reborn without end
from the Eternal.

December 20, 1951

Passed around by Ann Dasburg at Andrew's memorial

FOR M.

When I took your hand
two childhoods were married;
two continents enclosed with our names
merged and became one.
In your heart I found the secret treasures buried
by my child hand at the root of an ancient oak tree.
See! I said, showing my half of an old coin, broken.
And see! you answered, showing the half your hand held.
Then the days of our years burst into bloom around us
and we laughed with how time whirled in a bright ring
without end and without beginning.

December 1952

The "M" to whom this poem is addressed is May Sarton.

AUTUMN ON PILAR MOUNTAIN

My heart cries that we cannot walk together
this autumn on Pilar mountain.
Do you remember how the black slate
tipped upward layer upon layer,
how the sweat ran down our brows
as we climbed the last ridge,
and how good the apples tasted
we ate before we turned homeward?

We came back with our pockets full
of cruciform pebbles
the natives call "tears of Christ."
You explained to me then how molten rock cools
slowly to reveal its inner structure.
These crystals were dark as blood stains
and cold as burned-out stars
yet to me they reflected for an instant
everything man's eye has learned
to see in a cross form.
"The axes of a crystal"
are words that sing in my mind still.
Last summer's grass was golden
as we came down the mountain
you in your own world and I in mine,
yet both of us together
as earth and sun are.

September 24, 1953

POWAMU

A Hopi Ceremonial

The January moon has begun to wane in the winter sky.
In the Hopi kivas, I wonder,
do they begin the rites of Powamu?
Do men's hands and hearts prepare the fate of summer?

I think of the seeds buried now in the beds of moist sand.
I too watch over them. My heart is intent and waiting.
I make my mind dark. I listen as the seed does

to the word that cries Waken!
With my whole heart I seek this word,
with my will, with my wish,
like a mark aimed toward its arrow.
with the sensitive heart that has no ears, no eyesight.

61

The germ in the seed hears the cry of life
outside it, waiting.
Do they sing the seed from its darkness in the dark kivas?
When the moon is full will they dance
the triumph of living?

Will the Masked Powers move among men with gifts
and with chastisements?
Will the children learn it is men who must suffer
both good and evil
as well as embody it? On the Hopi mesas
will the wisdom of life be danced again at Powamu
under the silver and midnight sky?
Will the joy of renewed life
echo again in strong rhythms from the kivas?
Will it echo again in my heart that I may touch this
secret of wonder and power like the hem of a garment
in a crowded, unworshipping world?
Oh, God whose word has
been famine so long among men. I wait, I listen
for the prisoned seed to waken.

1954

THIS WAS A YEAR

This was a year of violence in our valley:
The madman, the murderer, the drowned child
haunt us still. There has been hunger among many;
the rains few. The earth does not yield as she used to.
Our bread comes to us sterile and from far off.
We do not break it with one another for a god's sake.
Some of our loved old have gone from us.
Our children, we say, do not honor us as they once did.
We have sometimes seen a jungle light in their young eyes.

I think, though, our time is not different from any other:
The sun shines upon us and the winds blow
good and evil among us as to all men.

Our hearts have often ached with another's anguish.
We have taken our friends' hands in joy.
Look, we have said at morning and evening,
Behold the mountain,
how the light upon it is holy! We have held the newborn
in our arms, the children of our children.
Their eyes look past us with an ancient wisdom.

December 1955

NANCY AT THE AIRPORT

Nancy in blue pants with bows at the knees
and a broad-brimmed bonnet;
her bottom's
sunflower round;
balanced by the fat belly, she's solid as a bean bag
and as full of beans, too;
hard to ride herd on as
a Texas dogie—
"What we need for this is a good cutting horse,"
we say at the end of an hour of it.
She loses herself in the forest of knees at the airport,
darts out of doorways,
scales stairs four-footed,
is ready to take off
on most anything for almost anywhere.
If it were a puppy we'd have it on a leash
or hidden in a basket.
A small human's
the despair of its mother,
two grandparents, and an aunt.
If we were three-eyed
and many-armed as Shiva
she would still escape us,
exploding with purpose in seventeen different directions
like a ripe fruit popping its seeds out.

Crossroads of the world,
international airport,
arrival, departure, this is her element.
Nancy's a bee in a meadow
zigzagging every which way.
Who knows what she stores up
in the round hive of her skull,
or if moment to moment rubs off
like pollen from a bee's back?
Would as soon take a plane for Afghanistan
as for Albuquerque;
set her down in China
she'll find a dog or a baby her size,
a chair to climb on,
a leaf to touch,
a corner to fall asleep in;
her nursery's everywhere.
Up she goes now into the bright air
in the steel belly of the monster;
what was our fairy-tale's her truth;
the flying carpet
will seem dull magic to her.
Goodbye, Nancy, God speed you
always among clouds, stars, mountain peaks and oceans.
Call down someday and tell us how the world looks
from the top tip of time's beanstalk!

1956

THURSDAY'S ROBYN'S BIRTHDAY

Goodness gracious sakes alive
can it be true that on *this* Thursday Robyn will be five?
It seems only day before yesterday that she was one
and that was hardly begun;
and I can remember how when she was very nearly three
she drove all the way to Taos
to spend Thanksgiving with me—

I mean she drove up with Uncle Hugh
and a lot of other college men
which I'm sure she'd rather look forward to
than back on when she is ten.
And when I think how twice five is ten
and four times five is twenty
it seems to me that right now five years is plenty.
It's just as well not to listen to too much arithmetic
because when the years gallop along too fast
it makes some people sea sick.
Besides it takes something more than arithmetic
to explain to me
how my birthday is just two days after Robyn's, yet on
      Saturday of 1956 *I'll* be fifty-three!

                            1956

I LIKE SAN FRANCISCO

I like San Francisco.
I like the way it's kind of warm and kind of cold
but never too much so;
kind of summer most of the time,
but kind of autumn almost every day.
I like the way the weather keeps on changing.
I like the way the fog moves
so it seems like something alive
floating among the treetops.
It's always doing funny things to the bridges,
kind of peek-a-boo things, like we do with children,
and we're like children, too. We burst out laughing
sometimes when the bridges
pop out at us from the fog
a little at a time, and then all at once suddenly
there or suddenly gone!

I like the way sometimes the wind
blows the blue morning around.

The clouds kind of gallop around the sky
with their tails in the air like horses.
I like the way the sky in the morning is sort of violet,
and the way the city shines up against it like a dream does.
Everything is sort of somehow Grecian
or how I think of Greece,
with the city so white and the blue bay all around it.

Time takes its own tail in its mouth so early in the morning
before today has really waked up yet.
It almost seems as though right now
might have been forever.

UNENDING

Up the steep stair at late night
and you in the small room wait.
I, wary of wandering, weary of love's interruptions,
longing to lie down beside you in the wide bed,
and the light of the lamp on the table warm around you
and the look of your eager loneliness and your long patience.

In the late evening of our joined lives we come together
as though a legendary journey were now ending;
all our false loves are stripped of their disguises,
as though I saw you for the first time in your true form,
as though you waked and found your dream beside you.

Why do I hesitate as my head longs
to home upon your shoulder?
I am like one who coming at long last on hidden treasure
cannot say the one word the gates must hear to open.
I lay me down in stubborn sleep beside you
and the long homeless dream begins once more,
the search not ended.

October 16-17, 1956

A GREETING

We've moved to a new house!
halfway up a hillside, forty-seven steps from the mailbox
and behind a thicket of pittosporum and pyracantha—
kind of evergreen shrubs they are,
lively with birds and berries.
We look over dark trees and bright ones,
like on the side of a canyon,
down, down to masses of white houses,
and beyond them the wide bay
and out through the Golden Gate
on clear days to the Pacific.
The sun and the moon set in glory over Tamalpais;
at night we look down into a jeweled darkness.

It's funny how this reminds me of Mesa Verde.
When I go down the steps each morning
to pick up the paper,
I think of the cliff cities perched under ledges of sandstone
the way we perch on the Berkeley hills,
the women going up and down to the spring for water
with their painted jars on their heads,
the children scrambling
naked as fish among the juniper and piñon,
the men off at daybreak to their hunting or their bean fields,
the old men asleep in the sun.
Time is really not so different;
the pattern of life repeats like a theme with variations.
The old cities were crowded, for their day, as our own are,
the future as uncertain; fear moves like a lean dog
among mankind; nothing we build lasts forever.
Nothing lasts but the light and shadow forever shifting
over the sea or the plain, the planets moving
in their grave dance; the stuff of which music is woven,
and laughter above all else that makes us human.

As they greeted the solstice each year at Mesa Verde,
the light that wakes in the heart as it does in the dark sky,
we greet it again in undying celebration,
looking upward from our city at the same stars.

Christmas 1957

CAT AND HUMMINGBIRD

The cat cries at my door.
The hummingbird warm in her mouth
drips fading colors of olive leaves and roses.
I cradle it in my hand:
the lifeless body
weighs less than a breath now.
Death has extinguished the bright eye
in which the world was mirrored.
From the beak black as a needle
the honeyed tongue drips like a tear.
The cat cries,
shut out of heaven.

June 23, 1959

PILGRIMAGE

The black stone:
I carried it all the way up the mountain.
When I came down,
a piece of the moon was shining in my pocket.

July 14, 1959

FOR HELEN GENTRY AND DAVID GREENHOOD

"Tis a most punctual, indeed a most industrious mouse
coming forth daily at 9.15 of the clock
to make a din of wastepaper quite the equal
of five matutinal trash men. The provident housewife
hath laid on poison but forebeareth to use it,
preferring to offer a modicum of tribute
for a modicum of chthonic entertainment.
She hath stored her flour in strong tins
and issued the order
said mouse is *not* to make lacework of the dishtowels
or else the truce is all off!"

November 1959

Chthonic = earthy–pronounced <u>th</u>*onic*
Helen Gentry and David Greenhood were friends
who came in for tea regularly.

THE GARDEN

She remembers
that when they cut down the pine tree
to make room for a road
she cried
as the saw chewed through the red bark
and the yellow flesh of the tree bled
its oils and odors on the clean air.

So when she returned
to the house belonging now to strangers,
a city with numbered streets
having taken the place of the forest,
and saw the fruit trees she had set out as seedlings,
the poplars beside the porch,

wisteria waving on the log wall
and the red roses by the door,
all now in the season of winter but
triumphantly alive still,
it seemed to her like a miracle.

She wondered what long-forgotten god
had kept the little garden
safe, a place to walk in
in the cool of the day, perhaps, lonely as leaf fall,
while the city spread and no one remembered Eden.

1959, after a visit to Los Alamos
New Mexico Quarterly

LETTER TO LUCIA

Lucia, it is you I remember more than anyone
in the Taos valley. You could not speak my language,
I, haltingly in yours, told you the daily duties.
    When you spoke of wind and weather,
of God, or of your children, I could understand a little.
    We made signs to each other and smiled,
or sometimes mingled quick tears as women do.
    The language of the heart is easy
and does not need what is taught in school.

You could not read nor write,
but I often envied the wisdom
you did not have to puzzle your head about.
    You trusted God and Our Lady.
Each spring the Passion was reenacted in your dooryard.
    The little Veronica dried the wooden tears
    of the life-size Christ in his red robes.

Juan, your half-blind husband
and a few old thin-faced men still keep the old ways,
   but the young do not, and,
   I think we both know, Lucia,
   that a time will die with them.

                    c. 1959

STAND THOU

Stand thou in the garden.
Stand.
The voice said, Stand;
play still-pond-no-more-moving.
I stood and questioned why?

Birds fly
and buttersfly
and flying carpets fly
and my young kitten almost flies;
then why not I?

Feet stand on ground.
Feet stand
still.
But bees fly back and forth
and comets fly
and kites fly in the wind
and summer flies
and winged words,
and even dragons fly.
Then why not I?

Must I stand still,
fenced in,
ringed round
in one small patch of ground
while time flies by
and fish and squirrels fly
and horses can have wings,
and angels, too,
and men and dogs go flying to the moon,
they tell us,
soon?

The voice said,
Stand
and see thou do His will.

His—not my own?
and must I try to stand as still as stone
and turn my thought
and all my senses in,
not hear, not see,
not be a bird—
just be?

1960s

*T*his decade of political murders ("For Jacqueline Kennedy"), in contrast, brought to the Churches more grandchildren ("Menagerie" and "Mockingbird"). But the suicide of a grandson and advancing years led to the contemplation of aging and mortality: Peggy's ideation of her own suicide was not too far from the surface, as expressed in "Temptation," but humor bubbled up in "The Let-Down" and "All Granma Wants." The "Anniversary" reveals a mature balance of understanding in the marriage. The dog in their lives, Poli, Poli-kota, "white butterfly" in Hopi, stimulated consideration of the connection between the animal and human worlds: " The Foxes Have Holes" and "Animal." Family distress ("For My Brother" and "The Sacrifice") resurfaced and was faced. "Sad Song" also chronicled a temporary setback, but personal tranquility returned. It was a solid period; a return to New Mexico, to roots in Santa Fe, with independent sons nearby and familiar mountains. There was time for wandering in the mountains and on the by-roads: "Owl by the Rio Grande," "Poem in October," and "Rio del Oso" align power and beauty in nature and express wonder at humanity's place. "For Such a Day" supports a foundation in the midst of chaos. The archetypal patterns Peggy's Jungian studies imprinted on her poetry emerge more and more strongly in these years as a result of study with an analyst in San Francisco and her on-going recording of her dreams.

TEMPTATION

Five stories up
I looked down on pavement
and envisioned the sudden end.

I had the power to
escape life.
Mash flesh to a mangle

of fractured bone,
to end this being
in a confusion of

split brains (Torn papers,
fragments of destruction
blew on the sodden wind.)

Lights in the
whirled rain glittered.
I stood in my live flesh

wishing an end to
this too vulnerable body.
Throw yourself down, the voice said,

have it over with in a minute.
But something greedier for
life said no,

and a kind of housewifely
objection to making a mess
on the anonymous pavement;

a feeling, too,
that to take one's own life
would be a kind of betrayal,

though who or what
was betrayed
I could not decipher.

I stood there for a long time,
the ragged curtain blowing.
The indifferent city noises
churned about me.

March 14, 1960

*Refers to a visit to the Embassy Hotel,
San Francisco, February 19-23, 1960.*

POEM FOR A CHRISTMAS CARD

I have gathered for you, for us both, another November
afternoon, walking up the late hill
among the granite crags.
Under my feet like fragments of frozen auroras
the small stones beam their many-angled
light, rose not yet become roses,
green not yet shaped into a calyx.
Where the rain has washed softer soil,
a deer's strong footprints.
The matted needles under a pine are trampled
like stable bedding and here and there are clawed tracks,
a scraping under of rocks, scooped holes
where paws or beaks have hunted
beetles or nuts or whatever
the sparse earth yields here.

Wandering, I track my own way upward.
The sleeping years awake and sing within me,
the winter air one with the airs of childhood;
a moon slips tilted up the blue sky.

November 23, 1960

*For many years Peggy composed poems like this as
Christmas greetings. A group of these were collected
in* A Rustle of Angels, *but several others are included here.*

EXILE

Exile:
Who knows whether from this world or
from some other, I
go looking for companions,
finding none to whom
the words I would speak have meaning.

STONES

Stones:
those many shaped small
smooth-polished pebbles
have been waiting so long
for the ear that can hear
how they cry out.

1963

MENAGERIE

The two little dark-haired girls
and the long-haired white dog
were playing together
round and round among the legs of tables
and the feet of adults perching
primly on chairs and sofas.
The two little girls
went over and over each other
like animated cushions
or flannel acrobats.
The white dog
bounded and licked their noses
with her pink tongue.
The young dog was as supple as rope,
the children almost,
except that not having tails
they fell down more often
and had a little more trouble
to pick themselves up again.
We grown-up people
sat about heavy as statues and
rigid as the bars of cages
enclosing an animal world.
Like spiders we kept spinning
nets of words to contain our creatures,
but over and over they escaped us
into dimensions we were always on the edge of
but could not get inside.

December 3, 1962

THE LET-DOWN

Something
Dante didn't imagine;
something
Becket hasn't got round yet
to presenting,
the hellish hour
trying to buy a brassiere to fit you
when your figure isn't the one any more
the designers see in their mind's eye
—or *you* even in *your* mind's.

Shut up in a little cubicle with a mirror
all too well lighted from overhead,
you stare at yourself as though
you were someone you'd rather not know.
You envy Hamlet
who wished that his solid flesh would melt.
Yours has;
at least it's no longer solid.
Your distinguishing feminine features
have become, let's face it,
more like an old hag's bags
than like a gazelle's twins.
The vinegar-faced dame who tried to fit you
fetches item after inadequate item, then says,
shaking her head, 'Dearie, you're so droopy
I just can't do anything for you."

You can understand now why
Adam and Eve might have been in such haste to
cover themselves with a drapery of fig leaves
if they'd eaten the apple
not in the blossom of their youth but
in their old age.

1963

FOR JACQUELINE KENNEDY, NOVEMBER 22-25, 1963

Out of the blue
the bolt came;
the split air
cracked;
the comfortable season
blackened.
Death strode onto the loud stage
in an instant Cain's hand
again cast doom.
Blood cried from the ground.
We stared aghast at hatred.

You gathered into your young hands
all our anguish and our sorrow.
You walked for us all
behind the bier of the day's joy.
You calmed the world by a light
that did not flicker in the worst storm.

Who was it taught you?
What spirit came to stand by you
in that moment when the roses you held
began to drip blood,
when your heart felt
clenched in the cruelest trap?
In this rough land,
America,
you suddenly shone like a true queen,
became marble constant
as Cleopatra in her dark hour.

However time may shake us
we can never forget this.
Something has waked in our hearts
that had slept too long.

We have seen the hero
borne from our own sad stage;
a passion has unfolded
before our living eyes.
This banal world
will never be the same.

Roses and blood;
the stain of one,
the beauty of the other
valiantly shown and known.
May we walk through the rest of this life
with greater courage
because of your gift to us, Jacqueline Kennedy.

December 1963

FRIGHTENED NIGHT

In the frightened night I lie sleepless;
the year strikes like a bad clock.
I know we are getting older.
Soon your age will be sixty-four.
I, too, am already sixty.
Time keeps going past us faster and faster.
Our children have long since outgrown us.
We live on in their quick world
like exiles who must be dumb
in an unknown language.
I do not feel the same joy
in watching the young leaves open.

Why should it surprise me
to find it so hard to face our separation?

Whenever you leave me
now I feel an unexpected
pang in my body's depths.
Can this be the beginning
of another sort of labor?
It is a long time since
I knew what it was to give birth.
Do we have to be *un*born
out of this sensual life
with as much pain?

1964

FOR MY BROTHER

Your letter, my brother,
is bleeding still in my hand,
the white page neatly typed and initialed
by the impersonal stenographer;
the letters abstract as Phoenician
could have no meaning for the stranger
to whom they were addressed,
but for me each word is a knife stabbed
into the fibers of my
sealed heart.

What was it, I wonder,
made you cry out to me
across the spent years?
Made you veil your cry,
sending me only the bare carbon
without signature or explanation?
Did you know I would hear
as your words burned
the voice of the lost child
crying still in nightmare?

ANNIVERSARY

Forty years married!
I dream someone gave me a ruby locket
that I keep hidden in my hand,
the time not yet ripe for me to wear it.

You give me a gold pin
that I pick out for myself
after endless window shopping
all about the city—
a round circle
with a cube dangling inside.
We both admire it.
We do not tell one another what we are thinking.

In the late summer
we go on a trip together
and fall in love all over again
with the river and the mountains.
I like exploring things.
You like knowing what they are made of.
We rejoice to see the clean stars
over us and to watch how the wild ducklings
move on the morning water.
At times we forget that we are growing older.

When we're at home I'm always fussing at you.
There's so much to be done.
The house keeps getting in between us.
Whatever you do for me
turns out half the time to be wrong.

The trouble, I think, is mostly
with the bosom friends who live
invisibly with and between us.
Yours is an accomplice
who delights to give wrong information;
mine a stiff female
who thinks she knows everything.

Unfinished, 1964

MOCKINGBIRD

For Julia

What is the mockingbird singing?
teaching me
words to make music with,
        words to make music;
not to say anything,
names calling nobody,
the sound of them only.

Davis! Davis! Davis!
Mary Jane! Mary Jane!
        Hurry up now! Hurry up now!
Come quickly. Come quickly. Come quickly.

Speed. Speed. Speed. Speed.
Cream and sugar, cream and sugar.
Galloping elephants. Galloping elephants.
        Teacher! Teacher!
        Come and find me. Come and Find me.
Wind it up now.
Speckled eggs, speckled eggs.
        Hemingway, Hemingway, Hemingway!

Bread'n'butter. Bread'n'butter.
Narrative, narrative, narrative.
        Sweep it. Sweep it.
Sweet peapod, sweet peapod, sweet peapod
Go to sleep. Go to sleep.
        Give it. Give it.
Jack it up! Jack it up.
        Never mind.

1964

SAD SONG

No one said
how it would be in our old age:
the terror of living
too long,
or of not living
which keeps on coming closer.

How many times have we
done these autumn chores?
Made the house tight
against another winter?

Now the house every day
is becoming our enemy.
It is the house that has joined us
so long. Now
whatever we share reminds us of separation,

leans on us heavier;
each year
seems to become colder.
We look more often on one another with strange eyes.

September 20, 1964

ALL GRANMA WANTS

All Granma wants for Christmas is a tree-toad,
a clean little green little tree-toad
with a gold chain and collar
so her it will foller
when she walks on the street or the free-road.

Granma hopes not one of her kin supposes
she might want nylons or a bunch of roses,
or a ring like some people wear in their ears
or their noses.

All she wants is a tree-toad;
just one of those so-hard-to-see toads
to sit on her shoulder
so all who behold her
will say, "Is that really a, Gee!–toad?"

This year Granma doesn't want a ride on an
el-ephant or an el-evator.
Don't give her an asphod-el,
not even one in a pot with a pretty smell!
She certainly hopes no one will possibly think
she'd like anything trimmed with mink.

No, all she wants is a tree-toad.
It can be either a lady or a he-toad
to sing and assuage
her for reaching such age
without having her own little glee-toad.

There are people who think
that nothing could be fina
than the Emperor's nightingale of China,
but don't send away for that; it would be a waste.
This granma doesn't have quite such a fancy taste.

All she has wanted since she was eight years old
is a dear little tree-toad to hold.
It would be too bad,
    don't you think, if she had to wait
    until she is ten times eight?

So sing hi! for the holly. Sing hi! for the pine.
Sing hi! for the house all mistletoed.
May the season bring
you each wished-for thing
but to Granma her own real tree-toad?

1964

OWL BY THE RIO GRANDE

From a cliff
above a bend in the river
an owl stared
like an old god watching
a galaxy he had just finished making.

He had tufted ears
a little like a feathered serpent's.
His eyes were two luminous dials;
his face a round wreath;
he was wreathed in a design of
leaves and fishes.

I felt a little embarrassed
to see him in afternoon's stern spotlight
so intent on another world,
as though I had intruded
into someone's room without knocking,
or by some accidental magic
opened the door into a different dimension
of time than the one we humans
are kept shut up in.

His unseeing eyes erased me.
Like the undressing of a woman
by a lewd glance he
divested the air of my presence
leaving me not at all sure
even of my own being.

Only the afternoon light seemed solid.
When the owl flew his great wings scooped it
into forms only Euclid could have spoken.

1965

RIO DEL OSO

Rio del Oso is the River of the Bear;
the sand is piled there
deeper than a sea-beach,
wide among hills that have
maybe buried mountains;
the threads of a thin stream
have managed to vanquish the poor road
in some other, wilder season.

We walked there yesterday
gazing at the gnawed remnants of a gone world,
could see beyond to
snow crests
under a sky as pure blue
as men can hardly remember,
so quiet
we were almost frightened by our own breath.

The dog ran about,
untroubled, as we were, by time's resonance,
caught a rat on a rock and tried to shake it
to an amazed death,

the only live thing
in the whole wilderness we saw
except a few birds,
so we felt we had to stop her.

As we walked back to the car
one of us found a worked fragment of red chert
that had lain there five hundred years at least
and could not tell us
whether its sharpened point had ever drawn blood.

1966

POEM IN OCTOBER

Gold
the river pours it
and blue—luminous—both
reveal light.

The unsubdued Rocky Mountains
lurch
against the far sky.

We
spread ourselves out on the grass.
The sun beats on us

as though our bones were
gold wire.

The birds have
almost all gone.
Only a few
ducks are warming themselves
together on a bare rock.

We are
faint with recalling the
lost trails
of animals and of men
who passed here
and will not come again.

Winters and summers
unwatched by any eye.

FOR SUCH A DAY

I.

How can I
talk of such a day?
Once or twice or
three times in a lifetime
come such, or is it we come upon them?
As entering by some
secret door in the mountain,
laying our hand by impulse on the rock face
it swings open.
We find ourselves a world where all is lighted
by shimmering jewel colors;
Or like those
Easter eggs of childhood
spun of white sugar—
We peer in wonder through the tiny peephole
and see a world in crystal.

II.

The year declining:
the sun glides
down the western sky.
All visionary heroes
sail to their western isle.

Walking down the western slope
of our mountain
in late afternoon
in autumn just past the equinox,
the night's dark
sends its long shadow upward.

III.

The dog runs ahead of us
white as a ghost or a pebble.
Everything else is color in the forest,
greens and deep blues,
touches of red on the late flowers,
browns,
a beginning of pale gold.
The dog dashes on mindless quests,
reads worlds
our sense cannot penetrate,
leaves urinal messages
at random perhaps,
but then,
how do we know?

Every now and then my own animal past stirs
in a language known long ago
and long forgotten.

THE SACRIFICE

Lion, golden as the fire we dream of in the earth's bowels,
fierce as a Van Gogh sun,
you raged through my childhood as my father's anger,
his unlived lust that was not allowed to become love.

The dainty thighs of my mother never learned to open
in joy. She was like the king's child
who sends her suitors on impossible expeditions.
He died a thousand times for her,
bringing her golden gifts and the tongues of dragons,
even his self, when she asked it, at last caged,
docile and bewildered, tame to the crack of the long whip.

How could I, a child, know what it was that padded
back and forth, back and forth
in the ribbed breast of my father,
the lightning that slept in his blind loins? Pity and terror
awoke too young in my dumb heart.

October 13, 14, 15

THE FOXES HAVE HOLES

The day we climbed among piñon, pine, and scrub oak
the rough back-side of the steep ridge
with the wind going high and over,
the city hidden
that spreads itself like a fungus on the earth's skin,
as the lichen does upon rocks and yet with beauty,

we came on a den of foxes dug under boulders,
a flat granite slab where my mind's eye saw them sunning,
the mother with young ones watching as bright as water.
There were thin black patches
of fecal stuff on the trail, and I guessed starvation
had been gnawing here this year.

The summer was rain-scant and the man-marred balance
between each kind and its prey makes it a thin thing
for creatures to stay alive.
I think the human spirit
famishes, too, cut off from the animal world it once shared.

The foxes have holes but fewer—
and where may a man walk
unfenced among mountains and wild things,
seeking vision?

> *Greetings from Ferm and Peggy Church*
> *Christmas 1967*

WORLD CRUMBLING

To stand still and feel the world you have known
crumbling like the shore under a child's foot;
an old tree by a dry wash,
you put your roots down a long way
to find water.
Now the floods come more often
the earth has tilted
a little;
the side of the arroyo eats back;
the exposed roots grope
under the sun's hot hand.
The water seems to rise higher
after each storm now.
The old tree's grip on the mountain
cannot hold in loose sand
much longer.
Time sifts slowly away in a trickle of prisms
and the red waters rage.

> *March 3, 1969*

FOR SOPHIE MENGIS, DEAD AT AGE 4

(from a news article)

How shall I live a little for Sophie Mengis
who was and is not, after a brief life?

Once when I was little
I lay on my stomach in a white house
cutting out valentines.
I had been sick with a cold
and had run away around the corner
in my bathrobe and slippers
because there was no one to play with.

There was a fire in the room
leaping with tongues as warm as kittens
and live as a song bird at the window.
I lay on my stomach on a fur rug
with a flannel nightie down to my feet
and millions of pieces of colored paper.
No one fussed at me to be careful
or chided the crumple of scraps
or kept on saying,
"Look out, you will cut your fingers."

There were scissors that opened their noses
as blunt as two crossed thumbs,
and miles of candy box lace.
Magic, to fold a paper,
cut it once in a curve and open!
Every time a heart shape,
Or hearts in a row like dancers.
There was paste to stick things together
and the tiniest paint brush to write
I love you! I love you!

1969

93

1970s

A certain peace had descended ("Alabado"), and a new dog, Baba, had come to live with them. Peggy began to reflect on her family and her life in "Praise for Feet." A book of poetry, *New and Selected Poems*, was brought out. She struggled with and finally abandoned a biography of Mary Austin. (Parts of that biography were published by Shelley Armitage as a companion to a work by Mary Austin in *Wind's Trail: The Early Life of Mary Austin* (Museum of New Mexico Press, 1990.) Peggy had found in Mary Austin a personality antithetical to all she was trying to achieve in her own emotional life and gave up on the unfinished biography. May Sarton ("After a Dream of May Sarton") was more compatible. The nature of evil as in "Kali" troubled her, but small pleasures ("Baba") balanced the anger. Long-time friendships were supportive, too, as in "A Few More Words for Virginia" and "August," which recalls time with Taos friend Corina Santistevan. Later, much of her work in this period centered on Fermor, documenting his illness—a brain tumor—his death, and the devastating loss she felt ("Years of Music"). Their marriage had been tried and tested and had triumphed. Her comfort was in nature ("The Landscapes") as it had always been, but the nature of death and the act of dying were evaluated ("Wednesday, January 29, 1973, p.m."). They had companioned one another through the years until he died seven months after their fiftieth wedding anniversary celebration. In sublimating her grief, she turned back to family ("Sister" and "Autobiographical Fragment") and nature. Finally, in "Notebook Jottings" she had come through.

ANIMAL

In the morning I wake.
My animal wakes up, too.
I feel it stir
half out of dream,
its head still curled between ambiguous paws.
Its eyes are closed.
The lightnings are unlit.
I must move gently lest I startle it.

My animal is only partly tame.
It comes and goes
of its own will, not mine,
and suffers me
the way I suffer it,
to share our common roof.
Its cave is deep
beneath the floor of sleep.

Sometimes I hear it roar
or howl
in its own dream.
Its muscles twitch
and frighten me with power.
What does it hunger for
that has been long extinct upon our earth? ...

Unfinished, April 1970

A FEW MORE WORDS FOR VIRGINIA

Virginia
has been re-arranging her treasures.
We are both at an age now
where it is no longer important
to march toward the future.
The horizon is a circle
that contains us
and all the places we have known.
The wide world traveled
has become the heart's inner treasure.

Whatever Virginia has known
is part of her—the geographical journeys,
the journey of her spirit
through the phases of woman's life,
loss and renewal,
the capacity to enjoy
brims over,
the water of life spilled
from the pitcher in the fairy tale in the hands of the princess
onto the dumb stones that sets them all to singing...

1970

*Addressed to Virginia Wirth Wiebenson, Peggy's Los
Alamos friend whose first husband's early death was
the subject of "Letter to Virginia" in* This Dancing
Ground of Sky.

AUGUST

August, a few hours with Corina
under the sun, the clouds—
the fragrance, the moisture of summer,
the world that is part of our flesh forever,
however long we may be absent—
moment of being
doubled in response—
a world affirmed
because we both have known it,
because for a few swift instants
we enter like children
the magic of a tree, a stone, a flower,
the silent surge of a landscape—
bearing our woman's wisdom
through grief and loss that is never really loss,
through death's shadow accepted,
—the cup,
the cup that our father hath given,
shall we not drink it?
—the bitter, the sweet of it,
—and the flowers that keep springing
out of the earth our tears have watered.

1970

PRAISE FOR FEET

Praise for these feet that have borne me
on so many errands and journeys,
the barefooted days among lilacs, the bee stings,
the stubbed toes, the bruises
of stones, of my horse's shod hoof when I was little.

Praise for the feel on my feet of grass in the morning,
the feathering touch of sea foam,
the gliding withdrawal of water
as the wave sucked outward,
the pleasant trickle of a brook in summer,
the sun-hot stones by the edge, the texture of rough rock.
The vein where an ankle was twisted shows blue still,
the shoe that had to be cut off
and my father coming all night
to change the cool compress,
he who had both the touch of a healer and of an assassin.
Praise for the calluses and blisters,
the long hikes, the mountain heights ascended,
the narrow trails and the steep ones,
the upward slopes without trails,
the hand holes and foot holes
made long ago in the rock face,
feet seeming to feel their own way
to follow as though wisdom came up
from the earth itself to guide them.

Praise for the rhythm of feet,
for the marching and waltzing,
for the double-quintuple
balance of toes,
for the whirling and leaping.
Praise for the lightness
of the upward spring
and for the delicate returning.

Praise for the architecture
of small bones, for the arches, for the roll of the ankle
for the rise on the ball of the foot as the racer leans forward,
for the spirit of Atalanta,
for the agile feet of girlhood.

Praise for the twined feet of lovers
for the shared warmth,
for the wordless communication,
for the knowledge of one another
that begins with the sole of the foot
and blossoms upward.
Praise then for the waxing belly,
the heaviness of the step,
the double burden,
the spread and brace of the foot bones
for the support of the feet in labor,
the push exerted upward
against the downward push
that wrenches the child forth.

Praise for the feel of the feet in slippers
on cold winter nights when a child cries
and the mother wakes to soothe it.
Praise for the countless footsteps of the housewife.

1971

KALI

Kali the heartless one.
Have we put her on the throne
in the place of God?
Or has she always been there
secretly aspiring
to take His vacant place?

She the mover to madness,
the crunching mandibles,
the caterpillar gnawing the leaf,
then the spider's grub
that has been skillfully stung
by the provident mother
into paralysis, not death,

the vital organs thriftily saved
to be the last crumb
of this larder of daily bread.

Life lives upon death.
This is her eternal and
unforgiving secret.
The robin racks the worm forth
that tills the earth
in industrious darkness
swallows it whole,
still writhing.
The cat is waiting for the robin.

The wolf slashes the tender underbelly
of the overtaken deer.
If the wolf fails
there is always cold for a weapon,
starvation and the glazed eye
to be plucked for a sweet delicacy
by the eagle.
Not a sparrow falls
but the fly or the beetle will grow fat.

There are angels, Blake thought,
who protect the tender nest.
The lion will guard the fold—from whom?
From the lion himself as Kali's beast?

The bloated carcasses
that once were men and women
float down the Mekong river
among the pleasure boats
and the puzzled fishes.

Oh, who hath done this deed?"
"Nobody. I myself. Farewell."

Out of the rotted hearts
in our still living flesh
the maggots crawl
and crawl,
take wings and fly
with promiscuous buzzing sounds.
The tongues with which we once
praised God
cry Fuck! or Shit!
The cage of our lost minds
emits an animal smell.

Is it Kali's will we do now, the dark destructress,
the mistress of swamps,
the avenging
mother of Furies,
sending us forth
and sending us forth again
on errands of unmercy?

In the beginning
the word was made flesh
and dwelt among us.
Out of words we, the makers,
made gods
who spoke
in poetic measures
and we heard them.

They were our power of making.
We who, from another time, remember
the beauty of speech, who still remember,
form the depth of our darkness, music,
who remember words and music,
hold our ears now to each other's hearts,
to each other's fucking heart.

Sorrow wrenches its way out,
sorrow and suffering.
Love and delight of which we once made music.
We stare at one another.
Our faces struggle to be human.

1971

Gus died
yesterday early morning.
His artist spirit
went free among the aspens,
his ninety years
shed in a shower of gold leaves.
On a day when
heaven lay all about
the angels made merry,
a kind of picnic for Gus,
a humorous ripple of harp strings.

October 9, 1971

*On the death of Gustave Baumann, woodcut
artist, painter, and carver*

BABA

I suppose it was madness
to bring home a new puppy
at our age,
one with such big paws
to grow up to,
her eyes as dark as mulberries,
opaque as one-way mirrors
she can see out through
but we cannot see behind.
She will not tell us
any of her secrets
no matter how we pretend we
always know exactly what she is thinking.
She, I feel certain,
is already on to us—
tries us out a little more each day,
or maybe tries herself out
to learn just how much animal
she will have to give up
in order to live so close to humans.

February 1971

AUTUMN

Autumn
sweeps us off our feet
too fast sometimes.
Exultation
once meant "to leap up,"
"to leap with joy."

There's something about the color of leaves in autumn
can set us raging
like the maenads who still live in us.
Fire-colored beasts come true.

I remember
getting out of my car once to gather oak leaves,
finding myself an eternity of moments later
leaping and twirling in a tawny thicket,
shouting on the amazed air, Tyger! Tyger!
in a voice I did not know was mine!

October 10, 1971

ALABADO

(Morning Song)

I behold the winter morning,
the leaf-fallen trees,
the mountain profile
serene through the chill air,
familiar morning
come round again,
return of a theme
in music.

I muffle myself
against cold in a green robe
and go about my duties
in the unawakened house;
dishes leap from cold slumber,
become warm,
I prepare the pattern of breakfast,
mystery of boiling water,
live fragrance of coffee,
the mute egg.

Before the dogs wake,
before the husband stirs,
like a priestess serving in
an ancient temple,
hands move through this ritual

at the edge of dark, of light,
the rise of morning
from sleep, from dream,
a perpetual
resurrection.

November 2, 1971

SKETCHBOOK 1972

*Peggy always carried a small notebook, a "sketchbook,"
in which she wrote short poems such as these. Her
longer poems were often composed in her journal,
which she wrote in every morning (in bed before
rising) and every evening.*

March 14

A red and blue kite
lashed to the highest branch
of a Chinese elm
hung there for now seven days
has turned to a pale ghost
the skeleton of last year's leaf
or the cast-off husk
of an old moon.

March 16

Spring comes
a smug cliché of fat buds
the earth is getting ready
to spring Spring upon us
the birds are making a racket
in the bland air
Why do I, growing old

in all this abundance of life
say to death, Move over;
Let us sit together a moment
on the doorstep?

March 24

In the morning
alone I feel myself welcoming
the goddess,
la divina,
older than a
stone in the stream,
younger than the sparkle of water,
clear mountain water
brimming under the rock,
so old and so young
I do not know how to
address her.
She smiles like St. Anne
in the painting by Leonardo
as I offer her the fragrance
of my morning cup of tea.
I see her eyes reflected
everywhere in the half light,
a very ancient companion,
a visitor whom I meet anew
each morning.
In her are all mysteries,
all deaths and
all survivals,
awareness of joy
and of heartbreak like the wave's withdrawal,
birth-pains,
the long slow struggle of bearing
each day as though there had been
no other.

AFTER A DREAM OF MAY SARTON

It is strange
that the book shelves in my dream
went upward stepwise, like an altar.
(Thus it forms itself
to the contemplative eye.)
The shelves set back in the center
could have been a tabernacle.
There, in the Jewish temple,
the scrolls of the law are kept.
But now in my dream
the book, both half hidden
and uplifted,
is a book by my poet friend,
or an article about her.
But no, I think it is her own,
a new one written,
as all her books are written,
in praise of the one goddess,
in praise, though she seldom names her,
of Aphrodite.

But now the signs of the goddess are visible
in this old and crumbling cathedral,
this Christian edifice,
the shells that have been her symbol
everywhere.
White shell
(we have found it even in the desert)
mysteriously lighted
the color of a sunset
or the petals of a rose.

On the adobe towers of a mission
formed of crumbling earth
she blossoms suddenly in shells
whose centers are roses,
roses that pulse with light
alive and glowing
on the edge of this nameless ruin—
our lady of presences,
our lady of transformations,
White Shell Woman,
Oh Mary virgin as snowfall.
Who comes now through the dark heaven
riding lowly upon an ass
to the place of annunciations.
The angel's hands reach
upward toward her
like the hands of a harp player.
The scene becomes golden
strands of an
unseen harp.
What hands are they, making music
of an old legend
on our dark night?

Poem handwritten into journal of March-June 1973

EPIGRAPH

Here I am
among pines and the sky
where I should be happy.
What is the meaning of this sense of absence
that will not let go my heart?

June 1975

THE LANDSCAPES

The landscapes
that I have traveled with you
catch at my heart so!
The campfires
you built with such patience
and such method;
the glades fringed by fir,
by aspen.

San Pedro
and the camp on the Chihuahueños
by Moses' Spring,
the lichen-covered
rock, and the lush wet
clods of green grass
where water bubbled up
around a hoof print;
the smell of saddle leather;
the sharp smell of sage and piñon.

The last camp
at Chaco Canyon,
the odyssey of planets
all night moving west
above the mesa.
You slept;
you were not with me.
In what disturbed dream
you lay I could not fathom—
Was this the beginning
already of your end?

Through this last year
little by little the woven fabric
of our life began to fray—
a thread here—one there—
nothing perceptible but
somehow you began withdrawing,
or were you being withdrawn?

That afternoon at Black Lake
when you left me alone,
forgotten within the mountain,
and I felt all at once how
it was to be alone;
some submerged force
had taken you from my side
and almost lost you.

Two spirits,
proud in their solitude's defense,
and yet so subtly,
joined in polarity,
Two poles attracting and repelling,
an inner resonance.

Death, the unraveler
tugs now at the mutual pattern,
I feel the tearing and scratching
of those rasping fingers.

So much is stored
within,
between us.

Yet I am the only one
who is still aware.

Happiness
of mountain mornings, the packed lunch,
the dogs
exuberant on their
individual pathways;
sherry drunk
in odd and sheltered corners
of granite,
of tall spruce meadows
looking downward
over the long familiar
valley,
wrinkled with light,
figured with passing shadow;
The Black Mesa,
Tunyo, like the square hub
of its own universe;
the slit of the river
like an explorer's map.

We have had so many heavenly moments.

November 1, 1974

*The Chihuahueños is a creek that flows out of the north end of the
Valles Caldera into the Rio Chama.*

WEDNESDAY, JANUARY 29, 1975 (P.M.)

I keep turning toward you
to ask you,
knowing that now there are no more answers;
you who were always responding
to my eager questions,
and to my questions that were only idle,
or sometimes aimed with malice like a thorn prick—
(women wear thorns on their fingers).

Even at the last when you could see almost nothing
I kept on asking,
"Where?"
"Do you perhaps remember?"
"Can you tell me what I should do now?"

I shall always feel sorrow when I remember
how you ruffled the dictionary
with such laborious searching
to find the word *psychiatry*
meaning *the curing of souls.*
It was almost the last thought
that aroused your sense of wonder.

YEARS OF MUSIC

So many years of music,
the strong thread
on which our years of strife
were woven.

This afternoon
while I was making bread
I played *Tosca* on the hi fi.
How many times did we hear it
sitting together at the Opera
under the windy
and star-blazed sky.
Tears burst through the cold crust
of my heart,
tears not yet wept
since the morning of your death.

My love,
your hand
still warm, clasping my own,
warm, strong and firm
as it ever was,
your hand on mine.
It was your hands I loved
always from the beginning,
your two good hands
holding and making,
guiding and reassuring.

It was your warm and living hand I felt
clasp mine as I knelt in church the other night
to await communion.
I had not performed this act
for thirty years. I felt alone
Like a ghost from my own past.

You and I had inhabited
this room of belief for half our married
lives; the familiar words were read
our minds no longer could accept,
yet an ember of faith,
what we two had learned to label faith
still smoldered;
not mind's belief,
not blind assent to doctrine or to laws,
only a sense of presence
shining through time, a living coal
in the ashes of the past
that blown on could still consume.

Are we not born to be consumed,
to feed this fire?

March 27-28, 1975

STONE INTO FLOWER

Death is not final. It has not taken you
far from my being, only beyond the sound
of my voice, of my touch when reaching toward you,
in daily life so seldom. I have found
your absence more a presence. The long labor
of love goes on, the impossible transformation
of seed into leaf into flower; the hidden color
of petal within the root—an impregnation
that cannot be reversed.

Spring 1975

PREMONITION

When you set out last year
to hike to the mountain called Bull of the Woods
you who seldom walk of your own accord
for pleasure and ignoring your knowledge that my feet
were good for only half the distance
suggested that I come, too, as usual on the picnic.
When I said I could not, you said you would go by yourself.
You had gone there on horseback some thirty years ago.
I should have taken warning
that something within you had gone awry.
Nevertheless, I only wondered a little
setting out beside you to go at least part way.
You kept leaving the trail to find out
what you thought was the best way.
I could see you plodding stolidly upward
and back away from the wild stream
that came frothing and chuckling
among sharp edged boulders
it had loosened from the cold mountain
and couldn't take time to wear down.
When the clouds began to come up
I said I had gone far enough
and would wait for you in the boggy little meadow.
You said then you, too, were tired
And would give up the wild whim
that had led you upward.

We ate lunch on a bare slope among rock cliffs
under a power line (how clear it all is to me still)
facing south, and you named the mountains for me.
(You were always quiet unless I asked you questions.)
This was a phase of your life you seldom spoke of
when you were still a teacher, a headmaster,
leading a troop of school boys up in the mountain.

You remembered, strangely, a girl you had encountered
riding once past your campfire—
a fragment of your dream world perhaps
engraved like the figures at Lascaux on the cave wall
in some deep recess of your life I had never entered.

We were worlds apart as we sat
side by side last summer on the mountain,
light years apart like the stars in a constellation
whose rays only now and then intersect.

When we came down you left
the trail again and went pathless
through thickets of rock and oak brush.
Perhaps you were even then "far wide" like King Lear
on the fringe of his madness.

September 1, 1975

SKETCHBOOK

How you would have loved this morning:
the mountains glazed with ice crystals,
their various curves and levels outlined in early light.
Steep ascents and levels invite my adventuring eye.
My heart leaps.
How quietly
you would have let it all drain inward
into the secret places of your being—
"the cistern contains. The fountain overflows."

And now I must leave you behind,
your essence among the ruins,
among the Ancestors,
and to do this, retrace my own steps backward
till I come at last to the days when
I forsook all alluring paths in my own nature,
all the tentative loves.

There are unlived fragments within me
still crying from their dungeons
in which they were cast,
unwindowed.

August 26, 1976

Written after the scattering of Ferm's ashes

DREAMING BACK

Loss aches within me when I remember
the things I always asked you to do for me,
the daily things;
my distress and sometimes my fury
because I had to ask you,
because you did not foresee my need;
asking you to walk the dog,
to clean up the dog yard,
to sweep the portals,
to trim the hedges and clip the vines,
to mow the grass
to pull the weeds.
"Why do I have to ask you over and over?"
How companionable we were
washing the dishes together
after every meal
and at table, when I read to you
and we played with words
out of dictionaries, as though they were games of cards.
And I wondered how women living alone
ever learned about their own shadows.

August 1975

AUGUST 23, 1976

We sat there all together,
hiding our common memories, if any,
our thoughts of life and of death.
The lidless eyes of the caves stared outward
in their encrusted silence,
caves waking a secret knowledge
among children—
the child I once was playing house among them,
picking up the pottery fragments
like words I had not learned how to read yet;
the arrowheads, the flaked chips
of agate and of hard flint
carried from far away,
fragments of a vanished life pattern,
the mysterious echoes
of the life that had once been lived here,
a life that had left no writing.

SISTER

Until *you* came
I had been the one and only;
played with, recited rhymes to,
scolded;
also the bone of contention
between mother and father:

Mother, who had grown up the one proud princess
in a family of rough boys,
married before she had finished with her childhood,

she, the descendent of a woman hanged for witchcraft,
of pioneer men who kept moving westward,
hungry for land, for cattle,
permitting none of their women to remain at peace long
beside any hearth fire or
tenderly planted fruit tree.
No wonder she always longed for the day
when she might queen it
in an ordered and settled place.

She married a blue-eyed wanderer
and became a mother too soon;
the instinct for cherishing
suddenly withered in her
like a bud nipped by frost
in its first blossom;
she suddenly turned into
the black-hearted stepmother of fairy tale,
the one who gave orders for the true bride's child to be
thrown away like a bundle of rags in the forest,
and its heart brought back as evidence by the huntsman.
Like us all she had been born with the two sides in her,
the yearning, the devouring.

Alas, I grew up in her image
and fulfilled my role as the unloved elder sister.
When you came along it was evident
you were the golden-haired true princess
whom all the princes in the realm would covet
for their sole and only.
You became instantly the Cinderella of our household.
Whether it was we made you thus
or whether it was fate implanted in you—
who knows or can ever guess?

May 5, 1976

121

CLIMBING UP

Climbing up
among the broken sticks,
the scattered long-dead branches,
the fragments of granite, the earth's bones
or the bones of another earth
that existed long before the time of this one
or of giants that once walked this earth
under a different air.
Trees grow now
out of collapsed rib cages;
their roots grip
along the under surface of skeletons
soil has never had time to cover.
Yet in the softer hollows
grass springs
and flowers at random,
delicate bluebells
and the leaning clusters of wild onion.

I came onto a ledge of rock,
granite, "A very hard igneous rock
usually gray or pink, consisting chiefly
of crystalline quartz, feldspar and mica."
The wind and weather
had not been able to disintegrate
this uplifted portion of earth's crust,
had worn it down some and flattened the surface a little.
There were a few niches
where seeds could take root.

It was spread like an ancient altar
bare to the sky, the crystalline nodules
refracted light in a dazzle of planes and angles,
the delicate aspen
leaves twinkled around its base.
From deep down
in the cleft of the mountains there came
the sound of water—
above, the sky was pure blue.
I found myself thinking somehow of Homer's Ida
not far from windy Troy,
a mountain of springs and forest
which the warriors of Greece defiled for their holocausts.
Homer had little love, I think, for those ranting heroes.

August 5, 1977

DECEMBER 9, 1977

Thinking of writing a poem, I cannot
any more trust myself to that element,
dive down into those depths.
I am afraid more and more
of the undertow,
the strong ebb of the sea drawn downward
along the steeping shore,
as if I again were a child
feeling the tug of the wave's decline around my ankles,
the immeasurable weight of water.

AUTOBIOGRAPHICAL FRAGMENT

My father gave me
a sensation of delighted terror
when he tossed me in his strong arms
and let the world drop out beneath me,
never once failing to catch me.
Never quite letting me drop on the hard earth.

Therefore I grew up fearing ladders and bridges,
dreaming at night of falling, falling
down bottomless sheer vistas.
How I envied the birds
whose feathered wings sustained them
on the steep slopes of the bright air!

My father gave me an eye for wide horizons,
my mother an eye for the comfortable enclosed room.
"I never liked windows with views," she said.
She planted shrubbery all around the house walls
and trees in thickets that would not let her see out.

My father gave me a strong horse and let me gallop
to the edges of everywhere,
to the edge of the clouds and the mountains.
My mother gave me a needle
and taught me how to thread it
and how to sew in little measured stitches.
From her I learned to fit intricate shapes together,
almost, until my father's ghost came tramping,
slamming doors behind him
and letting the vagabond wind in.

1978

AGING

When they were little
I was striding strong on my road
like the pioneer woman in the statue,
dragging my young by their hands
whose legs were not long enough yet to keep up.

Now it is I whose step is beginning to falter.
The distance between us is longer.
My children, my children's children,
almost out of sight now on a far horizon,
turn and call back.
It grows harder to understand them clearly.
I feel myself fall behind time that rushes past me.

*The statue is "Madonna of the Trail," one of a dozen
identical granite monuments created by the Daughters
of the American Revolution as memorials to pioneer
mothers. One of these is in Albuquerque, and another
is in Springerville, Arizona.*

DOUBLE HAIKU

I.

Raindrops froze quickly
last night on the bare branches;
by sunrise, ice bells!

II.

End of the next hour
nothing but empty circles
ring in the white snow.

AN ELEGY

It is not you alone for whom I weep;
it is all of life I weep for,
life rushing past me.
Music—sung and the song so soon ended;
voices we loved—and now gone
as though life kept rushing into another country,
life flowing past us
carrying blossoms, tree limbs,
rolling the stones over and over,
grinding them at last to the least dust;
moments of sorrow, moments of joy all gone past me;
spring here for only a single moment.

Kathleen Ferrier singing of love, of death
—death has taken her, too.
Does she exist, I wonder, "within the angel"—
Rilke's marvelous, invisible angel?

April 2, 1978

*Kathleen Ferrier (1912-1953), a Lancashire-born
contralto, was very popular in Britain.*

NOTEBOOK JOTTINGS

At five o'clock the white buddleia
is thick with butterflies and hummingbirds,
the white buddleia
cut down to its roots every year
rising unquenchable from the deep root,
bringing up from darkness
clusters of fragrant white,
white wands brimming with nectar,
wings folding and unfolding on every blossom.
A suspicion of angels
drifts into the dreaming roots.

March 23

When I wake up the morning becomes a poem.
Everything speaks of itself,
night's nightmare suspicions
dissolve, the bare branch
of wild plum in the crooked glass vase,
proclaims annunciation,
the piano
is pregnant with a universe of music.
My doubting fingers
translate the evidence of presence.

1980s

*T*he decade began with a surge of productivity. *A Rustle of Angels*, a collection of Christmas poems, was published in 1981. In 1985, *Birds of Daybreak*, a book of new poems, appeared. Many poems were worked out in her journals; her interest in her family and her past continued to be expressed in "Notes for an Autobiography" and "Of Flowers." Concerns about mortality were more immediate, personal, and real as she approached eighty ("On a Mountainside Yesterday" and "Stroke"). Her keen observations are apparent in "After Lying Awake," "How to Watch a Sunset," and "Lilacs." Then, in memories of her mother, a new understanding was reached, though the two had never been close ("Of Flowers" and "Notes for an Autobiography"). The question, "What do you think will happen?" and the poems, "Last Night the Moon" and "Death, Is It You?" came very close to providing a coda for Peggy's life. Certainly they do for this collection.

Some last works are missing, probably included in journals that were turned over to a Jungian analyst who helped Peggy develop and complete her plans for suicide, but who would not allow me access to them.

In October of 1986, Peggy Pond Church brought her life to an end, following the precepts of the Hemlock Society. She contacted each of her children's families, explaining and saying goodbye. The poet Haniel Long once said of Peggy, "...[P]erhaps she will be articulate in beauty past our generation's comprehension." He was correct; the beauty and the articulation are the obligation she left with me—the necessity of this volume.

SILENCE

Silence,
as though we were stones
at the lake's edge
the clear water ripples over
our separate beings,
touching us gently.
We become one for a time
with the movement of deep waters.

Silence.
We become so still,
yet something moves among us
when we leave off thinking,
when we dispense with wishing.
We feel the invisible
touch us with its own music.

April 29, 1981

LILACS

You can't just stare at the lilacs all the time,
shooting purple back at the sun,
tossing a purple surf like waves on a dry beach,
teaching the air to breathe purple.
You have to go on keeping up with your daily business,
hanging the wash out (Yes, I still hang the wash out!)
and taking it in again, straightening and folding it.
Washing the sticky dishes like a habit,
paying the bills, not just extracting the money
but doing the stubborn arithmetic,
signing the check, trying to remember
to put everything in the envelope and the right stamp on.
Take the dog for a walk,
noticing how all of a sudden the dry world is all green,
green for spring's sudden impatient moment,
with chords and cadenzas of lilac.

May 1981

POETRY

Poetry
inhabits the soul
like a secret animal,
inscrutable and golden
it accompanies my life,
has its own deep forest
where it roams and hides,
coming out only now and then
to sun itself in my garden,
withdrawn and demi-godlike,
will never become domestic,
comes and goes of its own free will.
If made too much of
will flee back into its forest
wild and intractable.

1982

THE WORLD CHANGED

The world you and I inhabited
no longer exists.
I think that last summer
was almost the end of it.
It was not your death that
made the difference;
the change had been going on for a long time.

The day of Pearl Harbor
when I realized our remote, our isolated mesa
was no longer beyond reach
of history.
Something in my bones knew it
though my mind was still unaware.
I still remember the afternoon
bright with sunlight that did not yet tremble.

March 2, 1982

OF FLOWERS

And suddenly this morning I wake
and find myself thinking
no longer of stones but
of flowers.

The earth is bare still
and cold
but last month a snow bank melted;
the blades of the iris were still green.

Last week I stole a branch
of bedraggled forsythia
that hung over a street wall.
Today the buds on the branch show a tinge of yellow.

I remember my mother taught me
to gather forsythia at the first hint
of spring when no other bush believed it
and house-warm it into bloom.

Spring came earlier than forsythia
in my mother's heart. The seed catalogs
brought it sooner than robins.
She sat in front of a log fire
turning the pages and dreaming

of wigelia, cotoneaster,
of gallardia and coreopsis,
of clusters of sweet peas,
of tall and rosy gladioli.

While I, her wild-hearted daughter,
scorned cultivated gardens
and waited impatiently for the pasque flowers
to bud on the stony hillsides,
flowers that had never been corralled in borders,
that grew where they alone knew how.

1982

APRIL 15, 1982

On the mountainside yesterday
all I could see was death.
Since I have been coming here
(a decade more or less)
the climate has been changing.
At first, walking with my young dog,
we could always find water
somewhere,
a thread of water
left over from snow or rainfall,
hidden among crevices,
cupped on a weathered surface.
But of late years no longer.
Seasons of drought have withered the mountainside;
tree roots searching the thin soil
choke on sand grains;
a young tree
has been rejected by its earth hold,
and, fallen, lies gasping
the way a fish does
pulled from its element.
Why do most of the pines have twisted branches
deformed as though some evil wind
had bent them?

APRIL 20, 1982

You can't dig up fossil pieces
of the soul.
Only sometimes
it reveals itself
in a drawing scratched on a hard rock,
flower pollen sifted
from an ancient grave,
a clay bird on the fragment of a clay pipe.

FRAGMENTS

This morning a dawn cloud
like a gravid female
fish swam up
toward the east,
streamlined as though moving against water.
Air is only another level of ocean.

January 24, 1983

We know that time is circular as February
leads us past Spring's beginning.
Early morning is already light-tinged.
In the east, the constellation Virgo has followed Orion
high over my left shoulder, glittering in brilliance.
My many years have been spent following the star courses
on the vast circle of my life,
the circles that dwindle each year,
growing smaller but complete still.
O, enormity in little—
How many angels
can dance on the head of a pin?

February 19, 1983

How to watch a sunset
without needing to put it into words?
Let it be quick
and be gone,
edged with its rainbow,
Palpitating with its
sheathed fire.

July 11, 1983

FROM 'NOTES FOR AN AUTOBIOGRAPHY"

My mother, whom I never saw naked
but once in a sudden illness,
alone,
he gone off to war,
and I, the tongue-tied eldest daughter
summoned to help with a back-rub,
pulling up her nightdress
and seeing the long scars at her waist,
"from the pins, used to hold our shirtwaists
inside our belts," she told me sighing.
To have been so scarred in the name of fashion
and never to have cried out!

March 10, 1983

STROKE

Helpless, I stand by
and watch an old friend suffer,
existing mindless in her ruined body.

I dare not bring her
the benison of a quick death.
It is life's cruel determination
that keeps her stretched on the rack,
denied release a hurt animal would be granted.

1983

AFTER LYING AWAKE

Cold,
not being able to warm myself
from inside.
Thinking how in old age
life becomes only a burden we long to slough off.
Thinking of my neighbor
exiled by ill health to live in Florida,
who loved flowers and skies and the
enticing shapes of birds
and adventure. Did you ever
get to ride in that hot air balloon, Evie?
Age closes us in.
The horizon grows tighter around us.
Sleepless till morning
I rose and pulled back the white drapes
from the east-facing picture window.
Oh, revelation!
Oh, brilliance of the dawn sky,
palpitant, rose over
ripples of pale gray.
I wish I could have called you, Evie,
to come and look with me.

July 30, 1983

FULL MOON IN FEBRUARY—MORNING

The moon hung in the western sky at dawn,
full-blown, a circle perfect
as Euclid might have dreamed.

The earth's rim
laden with mountains
moved upward past it
slowly,
making time visible.

I stood transfixed
in the air, shivering
as though I watched from the center of a dial
the measure of all measure.

No sound, not any pulse disturbed
that luminous motion.
That sense of earth, a great ship, drawn backward
into the light of yet another day.

1984

FOR YOU, MAY

For you, May, the muse has been everything,
a goddess in human form
many times worshipped and embraced,
flesh to warm human flesh—
the hand of a goddess that
wakens your inner music
so that flowers bloom
and wild beasts become still.
Even the briar that draws blood
also comes toward you singing.

My muse
has been only Narcissus in the pool,
never to be approached,
a speechless image
mirrored for me to gaze at
and interpret,
which sometimes shows me a Medusa's face
and the wild longing in Medusa's heart
to see herself human in my eyes.

December 16, 1984
(For May Sarton)

A WALK WITH YOUNG LOVERS

Walking with a pair of young lovers
through the tourist-infested town:
Greedy temples to Mammon
rise by mechanical crane like a false bird.

The lovers hold hands.
They are oblivious
to their raucous and irreverent
surroundings.

I stumble along beside them on my old feet
aching with too much time.
The river of years has swept me beyond the margins
of the world they are building between them.

July 24, 1985

DEATH, IS IT YOU?

Death, is it you I wonder
whose waxing presence like a dark moon
is driving me out of rest;
will not allow me
to sink into content
and slow cessation?
No longer can I cling to
my house as a refuge from you;
atom by atom
I see it being diminished.
Familiar objects
hung on walls that have long contained me
become impersonal,
become mere objects;
the walls dissolve behind them.
Windows no longer
frame a portion of outdoors
or close firmly to keep the winds out.
I become more naked
each day that I live.
The landscape out there is waiting to absorb me.
There is no cranny,
no chink in the walls that can hide me.
There is no one
in a safe room near by
I can call out to.
Only to me does my house appear in ruins.
No one else knows that I am the ghost that haunts it,
that daily my life is becoming an apparition
slowly released from time.
Oh Death, it is you whose presence
waxes within me as I wane.

It is you who must now be my constant study
like the score of unpracticed music,
a music in which I am waiting to be gathered,
a sound, a pure vibration
spreading like rings upon water where a fish leaps
once and returns,
leaving nothing behind but silence.

1984

LAST NIGHT THE MOON

Last night the moon—
light suddenly
flooding through my window
escaping a net
of dark clouds.

Over and over
our thoughts came to the brink
of death. An abyss
we could not cross with our blind words.

"What do you think will happen
to you after you die?"

"I think that's none of my business,"
I said quickly
and wondered why they all laughed sharply
as at a child who does not know
what he is saying.

I thought they might have understood better,
the Zen teacher and his students,
that attention to *one* life
at a time
is all that we are asked.

Would they have asked a river
what it thinks will happen
after it meets the sea?

August 29, 1985